Not Without Question

Written By: D.J. Brown

November Media Publishing, Chicago IL.

Copyright © 2019 D.J. Brown

All rights reserved. No part of this publication may be reproduced, distributed, or transmitted in any form or by any means, including photocopying, recording, or other electronic or mechanical methods, without the prior written permission of the publisher, except in the case of brief quotations embodied in critical reviews and certain other noncommercial uses permitted by copyright law. For permission requests, write to the publisher, addressed "Attention: Permissions Coordinator," at the email address below.

D.J. Brown
Indianapolis, IN 46220
djbrown@notwithoutquestion.com

Ordering Information: Special discounts are available on quantity purchases by corporations, associations, and others. For details, contact the publisher at the email address above.

Printed in the United States of America Produced & Published by November Media Publishing.

ISBN: 978-1-7326897-8-7

First Edition: February 2019

10 9 8 7 6 5 4 3 2

Dedicated to our mothers, with love: Pearline Williams and Myra Brown

Flowers for No Reason

A rainbow of colors like a scented sachet
A dozen or two to brighten your day
Roses pink and yellow and even red
To describe my feelings with no words said
Flowers for no reason a small thing to give
But let me give them anyway as long as I live
There is no special day, every day is heaven sent
There are many words I want to say to describe my intent
Here's a part of nature for your sight or to adorn
It's not just for the passing or the gift to one born
Here's to one so special
For each and every season
I think you deserve it, so here's flowers for no reason

~Arthur L. Williams Sr.

Contents

A Special Thanks vii

Prologue viii

Chapter 1: A New Beginning 1

Chapter 2: Rays of Hope 10

Chapter 3: Sunshiny Days 26

Chapter 4: Life As It Is 32

Chapter 5: The Right Tools 39

Chapter 6: Missing You! 52

Chapter 7: Follow Your Heart 60

Chapter 8: All Is Fair 66

Chapter 9: Wedding Plans 71

Chapter 10: Working Together 76

Chapter 11: The Course of Life 80

Chapter 12: Inseparable 90

Chapter 13: Season of Change 94

Chapter 14: Adjustments 102

Chapter 15: New Location 114

Chapter 16: Harmony? 124

Chapter 17: Searching...134

Chapter 18: Lifting the Fog 148

Chapter 19: Valued Times..154

Epilogue...168

Special Memories!! 170

A Special Thanks

Ron, you are the final touch added to my life so that I could start my journey with you. Thank you for loving me, believing in us, and letting me share my dreams with you.

Lisa and Latrice, I will treasure always the love, encouragement, and joy you give to my life each day. Thank you for everything. I love you both dearly.

Lee, Dora, Arthur, and Arnetta, thank you for your encouragement, for the support you give, and most of all for your love.

Margret, Carmen, Trina, Toni, Stephanie, and Daryl, I could not have asked for better sisters-in-law or a more loving brother-in-law in a marriage. Thank you for all your love and support.

Florence, Delores, and Jacqueline, thank you for your prayers and support. I love and appreciate all of you.

Thanks to Nancy Winters, Dr. Carolyn Peters, and Ever Lee. You have been an inspiration in my life for years. Continue to dream big and achieve your goals.

Prologue

"Mama, you should be a writer," Lisa said. "Latrice and I love to hear you tell stories."
"Lisa, what would I write about?"
"You and Ron always inspire people. Come sit at your computer. I know you can do it. Mama, write your story for us!"

The journeys in life. Each step and every move create more preconceived misconceptions. Journeys in which each turn presents obstacles, and the only way out is through perseverance, tears, and laughter— yield insight into the unknown complexities of life itself. Come, walk with me through the many challenges in life where each journey was not without question.

Chapter 1

A New Beginning

I opened the living room drapes to reveal the radiance of sunlight that peered through the window. *What a beautiful day!* I thought to myself as I stood there for a while, taking it all in. The birds were chirping in the shrubs right outside my front window, and what a lovely song they were singing on this gorgeous fall day.

I took another moment to enjoy the sunshine before heading into the kitchen to prepare for my oldest girl to come down so I could fix her hair. I turned the stove on and set the heavy comb on top of the low flames. Before long, she entered the kitchen and took a seat.

Children grow up so fast. . . . Lisa was in the fourth grade now. I was running the hot comb through her hair so I could style it in her favorite twist braids. I thought in maybe four more years, she'd probably want to wear curls all the time and wouldn't need my help for hardly anything to prepare for school. But I wouldn't think about that today. For now, I was just content to comb and twist her hair anyway she wanted.

I was startled when I heard soft laughter coming from my bedroom down the hall. The television was on a cartoon channel, and I could hear that my youngest, Latrice, was now awake and enjoying her morning shows. I thought she would have slept a little longer, but I was glad she had woken up on her own so she would be in a cheerful mood all day. I took note of Lisa's pleased expression as she played with the end of her hair and smiled. . . . We would all have a cheerful day. Before long, she was off to school, leaving Latrice and me to get ready for our day.

Today was my first day at my new job as a craft instructor at a local center. I would be shown the room I would work in as well as meet the staff and my new students. I was twenty-six years old, and I was so excited to finally be doing something I knew I would enjoy. I wanted to make sure I looked really nice on my first day, so the night before, I set the alarm clock an hour earlier than usual to give myself extra time in the morning. My navy-blue pantsuit paired with my long-sleeve silk navy and white blouse with red and gold brushed highlights was the perfect choice for my first day of teaching. The business casual was a bonus because I could remove my jacket if the room got too warm.

I finished with Lisa's hair and went about getting myself ready for the day. I dressed and took a moment to transfer everything from my black purse to my navy one, taking care to ensure I had my state identification card tucked safely in my wallet. I hung the shoulder bag on the closet doorknob and sat down on the edge of the bed. As I felt the time to leave getting closer, I couldn't help the nervous butterflies building in my stomach.

I slipped my shoes on, occupied with my thoughts. *Lord, what if the group I have to work with would prefer to work with someone else, or I am not the person they had in mind for their teacher?* I knew that sometimes I had to encourage myself, and this was definitely one of those days. I took a deep breath. *You can do it, Jean; you'll never know if you don't try!* I thought to myself.

I recalled my first meeting at the center several months ago. Latrice had gone with me because I didn't have a sitter. The center had sent one of its employees out to pick us up and said they would help me get transportation arranged for any upcoming visits I would need to make. We sat in the lobby for about ten minutes while Latrice read as much as she could to me from one of the magazines, quietly spelling aloud the words she didn't know. In the middle of a sentence, she jumped off my lap and ran to the other side of the room. I heard her ask someone with much excitement in her voice, "Are you Stevie Wonder?"

The man replied to her in a very calm, friendly voice and with a short laugh, "No, my name is Ron Brown, but I sure would like to have his money."

My daughter was sure she was right. "Uuh-huhnnn, you *are* Stevie Wonder."

"What's your name?" he asked.

"Latrice," she replied sweetly.

"What a pretty name!" he exclaimed.

"Come here, Latrice," I called to my daughter with my arms stretched out to grab her as I heard her running back towards me. Before I knew it, she was quickly on my lap again, asking, "Did you see Stevie, Mama?"

The man had stopped just long enough to talk to my daughter. He left, and all you could hear was the cane tapping on the tiled floor. A minute or two later, a voice from the desk in the waiting area called out to me. "Miss Jean, someone will see you now!"

It was a short meeting, and I was told they would give me a call as soon as everything was set up. "This is not a paid position, but we would really like to have an instructor on hand to give the students some guidance with their crafts."

"I'd love to, and I will be ready when you call!"

I left the center feeling exceptionally good and proud of myself for volunteering. I didn't need a paid position at this point in my life, despite my need to socialize and start feeling like the old Jean again. I had learned to use the gift that God gave me, and I was anxious to share that knowledge with others. Several months passed before I heard back from the center, and before I knew it, I was preparing for my first day.

Lisa was attending school full time, and I had made arrangements for Latrice to attend school on a half-day schedule. My aunt Lee was going to be at our home starting the next week. I felt so blessed to have her there because I knew Latrice would be well taken care of while I was volunteering at the center, which gave me a feeling of relief. But for now, she was content to accompany me throughout the day.

The doorbell rang at nine-thirty, and I was sure it was my ride. *Take a deep breath, girl, and calm down*, I said to myself as I walked to the side door of my home.

I opened the door and was pleased at the familiar voice of the visitor.

"Hello. Are you ready to get started?" David, my previous mobility instructor asked in greeting. He touched my arm lightly as I replied positively.

"Latrice, are you ready to go?"

"Yes, Mama!" She appeared at my side with her little purse that held her favorite nail polish colors and some coins, just in case there was a candy or bubble gum machine in the building. We could hear the coins' *ting*ing against the bottles of polish inside her purse as she swung it back and forth.

"You must be the baby girl," David said with a smile in his voice.

"Yes, I am," Latrice replied proudly, giving her purse another swing. The nail polishes clinked around again. My hairstylist, Ms. Bea, gave her nail polish each time we visited the salon. Ms. Bea would say, "My girl has to look pretty!" while showing her colors that were appropriate for a little girl her age.

Latrice would reply, "Thank you, Ms. Bea. Look, Mama, I got some more pretty colors!"

I would always smile and reply, "Just be careful with them, and make sure the top is screwed on tight!" Nail polish was always so hard to clean up.

I locked up the house, and David escorted us to the car. "How have you been, stranger?" I asked as I moved my cane across the sidewalk in front of me.

"I've been doing fine; just working hard," he replied.

When we reached the car, I took a moment to fold my cane up again and carefully touched the top of the door frame to make sure I didn't knock myself out while getting in the car. That wouldn't go over very well on the first day.

David opened the back door for Latrice, and she quickly said, "I can fasten my own seat belt."

But being a parent himself, he checked to make sure it was secure. It was. "Well, you are a big girl," he said, impressed as he closed both doors on the passenger side.

The ride to the center took only about twenty minutes, although it seemed much longer. David and I were catching up on the current events in our children's busy lives. It had been nearly a year since we had last seen each other. I had not talked to him since the training lessons in orientation and mobility ended. They were like all the other training sessions I had heard about for the blind that were just long enough to cover the basics. I worked with several different instructors, both male and female, on skills for the blind, but I didn't have a real connection with them that screamed out *friendship*. It was strictly training for me, and unless I passed one of them on the street, I would probably not see any of my instructors again. The training the center offered at the time wasn't something I wanted to do. I had mixed emotions about everything that I was being forced to deal with, and I couldn't see how any of it was going to benefit me.

The lack of training for the blind was a major problem. There were no high expectations for a person with very little vision or a person who didn't have any vision at all. I knew I wanted to make a difference, not just in my life but in the lives of other people who were blind. I had no idea where to start or how long it would take, but I had to have something to offer this new way of life. There had to be someone just like me who didn't know they would one day be blind, someone just like me who didn't know they would have to live in the same space as others and unable to view it with clarity. There were days that were good, but others left me fearful.

Several weeks prior to applying for the craft instructor position, I began the mobility lessons, where I met David. I knew for certain that being blind made me want to trust everyone just in case I needed to ask a question or needed some assistance. I found out during one of our lessons that I had to be careful of my surroundings even more now than ever before when an older guy reached out from within the doorway of an abandoned building and grabbed me.

David, following a little more than half a block away, ran as fast as he could to help me. "Leave her alone! Let her go!" he yelled.

The guy let go of my arm and escaped back into the building. As fast as he had appeared, he seemed to disappear. With tears falling down my face, I stood there feeling so afraid, wondering if this was what I should expect to happen. *Will I ever be able to walk down a street alone again?*

I had so many questions.... There had to be a better way of life, one without all the fear and distrust. As we walked back to the car after that ordeal, I remember wishing a strong wind would come through and take away the smell of what I was sure had to be alcohol from the old man breathing all over my face. David said he looked really dirty, so maybe it wasn't all alcohol I smelled. I was just afraid that if such an attack ever happened again, I wouldn't be so lucky. I wondered what I would do if my mobility instructor wasn't less than a block behind me. What would I do then? I just knew that if it happened again, I would fight for my life and make my assailant think he had found a five-foot-seven, one-hundred-eighteen-pound woman who was going to give him a little bit of hell right here on earth. The thought of my fighting with someone brought a smile to my face, but it was quickly replaced by fear. I gave some serious thought to where I would have liked to have put my foot or what object I could have swung to cause him great pain and allow me to defend myself. Thankfully, after more classes and training, I felt surer of myself, but I would avoid any repeats if I could help it.

As soon as we entered the building, David started introducing me to people at the front desk. Some of them were staff, and others were clients who received training at the center. While we were walking through the building, David told me there was someone he wanted me to meet. As we left the waiting area, he said, "Here comes my friend now. I think you'll like him."

The two men greeted each other, and then Latrice and I were introduced to Ron. However, Latrice certainly had not forgotten who he was and immediately exclaimed, "Mama, it's Stevie again!"

I'm sure he smiled. "Follow me, young lady, and I'll show you where your mom will be working," he replied.

Ron was a tall man with a personality that seemed to scream, *I'm confident, witty, and quite the conversationalist.* He used a cane too and walked with long strides through the building. Whenever he touched someone, he quickly said, "Excuse me," and kept moving with the same *tap, tap* rhyme as if he didn't want to interrupt his rhythm. I also used a cane, but the difference in my technique and his were amazing to me. Yes, he definitely had confidence. I walked with my left hand touching David's arm. We went down a long hall, made a right turn, and then went down a short hallway, where we made a left turn once we had gone through the double doors. I was trying hard to remember each step so I could familiarize myself with the building. It was very important to me that I appeared to be totally self-sufficient.

This was my first position since I had lost my sight, and I was not sure of myself at all, at least not as a blind person. However, I did put on a good front; I had everything figured out. If there was something someone wanted to make and I didn't know how, I simply would say, "That sounds like something we may be able to work on in a couple of weeks." That would allow me the time to go home and teach myself so I would be prepared for the upcoming lesson.

First we would build birdhouses. Each little birdhouse had several pieces that needed to be assembled, starting from the bottom and going all the way up to the roof. All of the pieces had grooves that held another piece in place, and this was the perfect project to build my students' confidence level in themselves.

Most of my students hadn't tried to assemble anything as a blind person, and it was my job to let them know they could do it. I would say, "Picture it in your mind, and then build that image; it can all be done using your sense of touch." I constantly reminded them that nothing they were going to do in my class required sight.

The next craft would be a little more difficult, and some projects would take more than two lessons to complete. I figured that soon I would find out just how enthused my group would be to learn these crafts and even more how those who had some sight would accept a blind person as their instructor.

***

I was checking out the inventory that was stored in a large basket when I realized Latrice was no longer in the room.

"Has anyone seem my daughter?" I asked the room.

Donna, one of my students, replied, "Oh, she's with Ron. But don't worry; he won't let anything happen to her."

I couldn't believe what she had just said, and it bothered me that she would knowingly let him take her out of the room. "Can you tell me where I need to go to find them?"

She directed me to the cafeteria, and as I approached the flight of stairs, I could hear the two of them talking.

"So, you are four going on twenty-four?" Ron asked with a chuckle.

He knew she didn't understand what he meant when she replied, "No, I'm just four."

They were sitting at one of the tables and looked surprised when they caught sight of me. It was clear that my child was alright, so as calmly as possible, I addressed my daughter. "Young lady, remember that you are never to leave without telling me where you are going, and never leave with a stranger,"

"I'm sorry, Mama, but Mr. Ron said he would get me lunch because I was hungry," Latrice replied sheepishly.

I turned to face him and addressed the other adult. "So, Mr. Ron, what is she having for lunch?"

This little tiny child thought she could actually eat a honey bun, a Snickers bar, one roll of Life Savers, a bag of chips, cookies, and a carton of milk, and what's even worse…an adult had bought it for her. I leaned over, placing one hand on the table, and said to Mr. Ron in a low voice, "If my child has a stomachache tonight, I'll be calling you."

His tone told me he had a smirk on his face as he replied, "That's fine with me. Would you like my number?"

I turned from his side of the table to face my child and moved quickly in my frustration to help her gather up her bundle of goodies. I asked her if she had thanked Mr. Ron, to which she replied, "Yes."

I turned to Ron. "Thank you for her snacks. It is her lunchtime, but please let me know when you want to take her out of the room."

As we were walking away, he replied, "I just didn't want to interrupt your meeting. I really didn't mean to scare you." The tone of his voice was softer, and he sounded very sincere. I almost apologized, but I would have said the same thing to anyone, so I just thanked him again for keeping an eye on her.

"You're welcome, Jeannie," he replied in a very thoughtful tone.

We returned to the craft room, and Latrice sat on the tall stool with the high back and enjoyed all the attention everyone in the group gave her. To my amazement, when it was time to leave, she wanted to know if she could take Mr. Ron home. I kept the answer simple. The response was "No."

Chapter 2

Rays of Hope

Ron and I had been talking every week for over a month at the center when he asked me for my phone number, which led to a conversation I didn't want to have with anyone.

"I just got a divorce, I have two daughters, and I really don't think I'm ready to start the dating game again so soon," I explained.

He just smiled and replied smoothly, "Then we won't date. I'll just be your friend." He seemed to be so sure of himself, laughing and joking around as if he didn't have a care in the world. How could I resist a conversation with a guy with so much personality?

"Jean, you've got to let your hair down sometimes," he commented and then asked if I liked to dance.

I was taken aback. "Yes, I do."

"Good. Then one day we'll go out and have a little fun, whenever you're ready. But I'd better get back to work, girl. You'll make a brother lose his job." He chuckled.

"Oh no, don't do that," I said, and we both laughed as he made his way out of the craft room.

I wasn't very sure about a lot of things in my life at that time, but I knew this was one guy I didn't want to shut out before I got to know him better. Ron would sit in on my lessons whenever he could, pretending he had an interest in learning crafts while he teased with some of the students and held more serious conversations with others, making his entrance in and out of the craft area several times during my short time there each week.

It soon became quite apparent that crafts were not what Ron had an interest in. Every chance he got without stepping out of line as a professional, he would go out of his way to compliment me. "Your perfume smells really nice," he would say. Once he touched my hair while standing behind my stool and exclaimed, "Dang! You got some long, pretty hair."

I was quiet in a way, but I knew one day he would want to check me out, and whenever he did, I wanted to give him an image he wouldn't forget. Both of us knew our conversations probably should have been much shorter and less flirtatious at work, but every encounter told me I wanted to know him better.

"I know a little boy who needs someplace to go for Thanksgiving Day dinner. Do you mind having a guest? I'm sure you'll like him," he asked nicely. Obviously, he had been standing in the room while I was talking to one of the students about our family dinner.

I thought about it. "No, I don't mind, but how will he get to my house?"

"Oh, don't worry. I'll make sure he gets there. I'll be there at three-thirty," he replied with a grin. Of course, there was no little homeless boy, but there was Ron, and his intentions were to get invited to my house for dinner, and so he did.

When Thanksgiving arrived, I had prepared a meal fit for royalty. Latrice had folded the napkins while Lisa placed the silverware on each one and put a glass at the top right of each napkin as she had been instructed.

"Mama, we did it just like you told us to!" they said proudly.

"You two set the table like a couple of experts," I replied as I walked around the table to make sure it was perfect. The centerpiece was not going to be a floral arrangement this year; instead I had made a sweet potato casserole that had a metal cup in the center that was half filled with a shot glass of brandy. I sat it on the table just as the family arrived, only to have to remove it from the table and put it back in the oven to keep it warm while we waited for Ron to arrive.

Eventually, after we had taken plenty of time catching up and putting off dinner, my mama asked, "Jean, do you want me to go and pick him up?"

I could only shrug. "I don't know where he is. I've tried to call him, but there is no answer."

There had to be a look of confusion on my face as I paused for a moment to think about what I should do. The man certainly had me puzzled and quite irritated with him. "Maybe he changed his mind?" I turned to my aunt Lee. "Will you go ahead and light the brandy? It's getting late. I'm going to fix the plates now."

All I felt was disappointment on a day that was usually filled with stress-free conversations and laughter that filled the house. I didn't know what to say to my family when Ron didn't show up. I was totally embarrassed, especially after holding up everything for over an hour. I had been stood up, and all I knew was it would never happen again, at least not by him! His smooth talk had gotten him the invite, but it was for nothing more than dinner, and what were the chances of my inviting him ever again?

We gathered around the dining room table, where we held hands and Mama said the grace, thanking the Lord for our family and all the blessings He had given us. Mama's bone cancer was still in remission. Dora and her three children were now with us, so Mama had all her children close by except our brother, Arthur, his beautiful wife, and their four children. Aunt Lee didn't have any children, but she had a very special bond with all her nieces and nephews that assured each one of us that we could count on her to be there for us no matter what the situation, and we loved her even more for that. We played games, listened to music, talked, and wrapped plates to go when we finished eating dinner.

I spoke aloud softly. "Yes, Lord, thank you for all the love you have surrounded us with from generation to generation." All in all, while I was still sour about Ron standing me up, I was happy to be surrounded by all my family and sad to see them all part ways at the end of the evening.

My phone rang, and when I answered and heard Ron's voice, I was surprised yet still very angry. "So you remembered my phone number. You would have thought that when Alexander Graham Bell invented the telephone, he only made one and I own it! How do you just not show up? You invite yourself and have the nerve to be a no-show? What were you thinking?"

After my series of questions, Ron managed to get a word in. "I'm sorry. It won't happen again, but I couldn't get a ride. I'm leaving home now if I can still come over. I can be there in twenty-five minutes. I'll see you then."

All of a sudden, I was listening to a dial tone. I took the phone from my ear and looked at it. "What the . . . ? I don't believe he hung up on me!" I put the receiver on the wall base and continued to clean my kitchen. I thought to myself, *Well, this little friendship is going nowhere fast.* I just couldn't figure out why he had lied to me. I wondered, *Did he just want to see if I would say yes? Is this some game single men play?* Well, for the first time, he had rubbed me the wrong way, and I was going to let him know it as soon as I received a phone call from him.

I would have called my best friend, Delores, but I thought about the day I'd called her when I was angry with my children's father and she told me, "I'm on my way over there." She arrived at the house in a very short time and was ready to go. "Let's go. Get your boots and coat on. Come on," she said while rushing me out of the house.

We started walking, and I asked her where she had parked the car. She replied, "You don't need the car. All you need is this cool breeze to cool you off a little bit." Had she lost her mind? It wasn't cool outside; it was cold! I don't know how long we were out there walking, but I think I forgot what I was so angry about by the time she finished talking to me and making me freeze my buns off.

When I got back home, I thought, *You've got to love her tactics!*

I decided against calling Delores. *Just finish cleaning up. There's no need to tell her how angry I am, and I'm too tired to walk anywhere.*

I heard a car door slam in front of the house, and a few seconds later my doorbell was ringing. I folded the drying towel and hung it on the towel rack.

"Yes?" I called out.

He replied, "It's Ron. I come with a peace offering." I opened the door, and he said, "I'm really sorry. Do I need to toss my hat in first?" He had a bag in his hand. He reached into it and pulled out a bottle of white Zinfandel, which was my favorite white wine. "I bought the girls a bottle of Orange Crush and some chips we can all share—that is, if you don't mind having company for a while," he added.

I shook my head, took a deep breath, and replied, "Come on in, and thank you for the peace offering."

The girls chimed in, saying, "Thank you, Mr. Ron." They turned to me. "Mama, may we stay up and watch TV too?"

Since it was a holiday weekend, I agreed. I went to the kitchen for glasses. Ron followed behind me, asking if he could open the wine for me.

"Yes, that would be nice."

Ron filled the glasses generously while I did the honors of filling two more with orange soda. We joined the girls on the floor, and for the next couple of hours, we had fun watching a comedy. For the first time in a long time, the girls and I truly felt safe and secure. We had not had any trouble at home, but because we were there alone every night since the divorce, I felt as if I needed to listen for every sound as it might have been an intruder. The nights were too long, and my fear of what might have been lurking on the other side of my door frightened me. I had always heard that most crimes were committed in the middle of the night, and now I found myself staying awake much too late and praying, "Lord, help me protect my daughters. If ever anything happens, let them be safe."

It was nice to have someone to talk to. Ron was so full of life and energy that his blindness didn't matter to me at all. I had met a few guys after the divorce and had to ask myself, *What in the world am I doing?* No one had been my type so far. I'd met a functional alcoholic, a guy who thought he had to be the topic of all conversations, and a married player who had no desire to be truthful to anyone. It was a pleasure to hold an intelligent conversation with someone, watch a movie, or just share the experiences of the day with each other. My evenings were rather quiet when the girls were asleep, and many nights

I stayed up working on leather or macramé craft orders. It would be safe to say my life wasn't bubbling over with excitement, and it seemed to me that one day just simply rolled into the next as a different day but with the same complexities. I didn't need my life to read like a fairy tale, but I did need to be able to turn the page so I could move forward.

When I met Ron, my biggest concern about our relationship wasn't about our blindness but what my two young girls would be thinking. Would they think I was trying to replace their dad by inviting another man to our home? Even though the divorce was final, I wondered if they understood what that meant. I did not want to do anything to upset them emotionally or to jeopardize their security, so I thought I would take it really slow and follow their lead because we were in this together. They were the joy of my life, and I knew that even without my sight, I had to make my daughters see that I had done all I could to provide for them. It wasn't going to be easy, but I had to let go of the past and move ahead with my life. Being surrounded by my imaginary brick wall was making me spend too much precious time dwelling on what could or should have been different. I would never have a relationship with anyone if I didn't let my guard down enough to let someone in.

***

I walked carefully down the flight of stairs at the center the following week, swiping the cane across each step to make sure nothing was there to trip me. I walked with caution in this area because you never knew when someone would be heading in your direction with a cup of coffee or a lunch tray. I wanted to get a snack from the vending machines. At least three women were standing at the pop machine, two discussing the selections.

"Could you tell me if there are any M&M's with peanuts and how much they are?" I asked.

"I'll push the button for you. Just put in a dollar," one of the ladies replied. I was grateful to get help so I wouldn't be late going to the work area.

Ron came out of his office looking for me. I could hear him asking someone, "Do you know if Jean is here yet?"

"Yes. She's at the vending machines," someone answered.

"Jean?" he called over to me from across the room while still using his cane to maneuver around the tables and chairs in the lunchroom.

"I'm over here," I replied.

"I want to give you something. Grab a wing," he said as he extended his arm for me to take. "I'll guide you to my office." Turning to go back in the direction he had come from, he offered me his right arm and said, "Watch for landmarks, Jean. it will help you get around easier." He went on to explain, "Things that are always in the same place can help you get your bearings, especially in a large building . . . like that trash can, 'cause it's always there," he said as he tapped the metal trash can with the tip of his cane. It made a sharp *ting*, and we continued to walk to his office.

"Alright, I will. Thank you for helping me learn my way around." I had always had this fear of entering a door and having it shut behind me, and no one would know where I was. It was a silly thought, but being blind made me aware of some fears I never knew I had.

The tall, slim man had a soothing voice that was calming. "Not a problem."

As soon as we entered the small office, Ron said, "There are a desk, two chairs, and a file cabinet in here. Always be aware of your surroundings. That is the key to finding your way around." He reached over on the desk and handed me a box. "This is for you," he said.

I opened it to find my first braille watch. I was surprised that I had a gift but was also confused because I had no idea how to tell time on a watch that I couldn't see. "It's so nice," I said.

Ron took the box from me and said, "I'll show you how to read it."

I had been blind for four years and had never owned a watch I didn't have to show to someone else so they could look at it and tell me the time. It was then that I breathed a sigh of relief as Ron showed me the braille under the face that opened so I could put my finger inside it.

"You shouldn't have to ask what time it is. You've got to know so you can end your lessons on time" he said.

I hadn't thought about that, but I was glad he had. He took the watch out of the case and offered to help me put it on.

"Ron, it's a perfect fit. Thank you!" I exclaimed as I looked at him warmly even though he didn't know it . . . or did he? Could he tell how pleased I was by the tone of my voice? I certainly could tell he was a very thoughtful man who was trying to please me. The question in my mind was, why?

Our conversations during the day were brief because he was at work, but in the evening we could talk as long as we wanted. Some nights the phone would ring, and, trying hard not to wake the girls, I would take the phone from my bedroom to the living room, and we would talk for hours. We talked about the relationship I had with Mama and of the love we shared. There was nothing she wouldn't do for her children. It was hard for her to find work that paid enough to take care of us, but she always managed to make ends meet with a little left over for some fun. She had a bad heart, diabetes, and bone cancer, which was in remission right then. She was a tough cookie, though. Mama had been sick most of her life, but it never stopped her from doing everything possible for us; we never went without and couldn't have asked for a better mom.

"Now tell me about your mother," I said.

Ron replied, "Well, I'll say this about my mother: she's a strong woman. When I lost my sight, she made sure I didn't give up on myself." Ron went on to say, "There would be no long-term pity parties in her house, and I'm so glad she had the strength I needed to build me up mentally. I think that once I lost my sight and accepted the fact that it was gone and never coming back, I had to prove to my family I could make it and that I wouldn't be a burden to anyone".

"Yeah, I know what you mean. . . . Mama has been my strength through this whole ordeal." I took a sip of my hot tea and sat on the stool in the kitchen.

"How did our mothers get to be so strong?" Ron asked.

"I don't know, but a lot of mothers would have said, 'This is too much for me to deal with,' and sent their child away. It would be a shame to do that and miss out on the blessings that child could bring to their lives." After a moment I said, "You know, the doctors said that if I had a son, the chances of him being blind would be very great, and they may be right, but it wouldn't matter. I would take that chance and make sure he got all the training possible, and just like my daughters, I would be there to love him through all the good and bad times."

***

Each week gave me something to look forward to at the center. It was an environment that offered braille, cooking, and orientation and mobility lessons.

"Learning braille will make things easier for you. Just think of how much you will be able to help your children and even take notes for yourself. If you need to write down a phone number or address, who will do it for you?" The braille instructor was telling me how learning the system would make my life so much easier.

Her office seemed to be filled with books to teach from in grade one and two braille. She was very pleasant, but after sitting at the small, round table for almost an hour, I realized I didn't want to learn braille. It all seemed so complicated trying to convert the print to this series of dots that were supposed to represent letters and numbers that I had read all my life. I was very adamant about it; I was not going to read if it meant feeling a page covered with bumps. No, not me!

"Thank you for your time," I said to the instructor. "Maybe we can do this at a later date."

I was sliding my chair back so I could stand up to leave when her very calm, yet assertive voice said, "My door is always open. Please come back whenever you are ready. Braille is not the easiest thing to learn, but believe me, one day you will want to learn."

"I'm just not ready, but thank you," I said as I turned to leave.

Now here I was back in the very same building with people who had trained me, or had at least tried to.

I had been given a small stack of braille paper, a slate, and a stylus when I had first lost my sight. "This is what you will need to learn to write with," I was told.

The paper was to be placed between the two pieces of metal with the open squares on the top. Once it was closed, all letters, numbers, and punctuation marks were to be written in the square, which I learned was called a *cell*. Each one of the cells had six dots, and anything could be written with the use of the stylus. This was like writing in a foreign language. Everything was written in reverse, and the margin started on the right-hand side of the page; you wrote from the right side to the left. Once I had finished writing, I would have to turn the page over to read the braille. I remember the first sentence I tried to write was, "I am so confused." The little stylus tool was used to make the series of dots on the paper; however, this process seemed to try my patience, and my pride told me I could make it through life without braille.

Where did the time go? I was given a braille writer by the Lions Club. There was only one problem. I had not gotten the training I needed to obtain the speed or accuracy to be able to read a page and not lose my train of thought. At least two or three days a week, I went to the dining room table with my writer and paper to try to accomplish writing anything correctly, only to try to read it with about sixty percent of it written incorrectly. It was obvious this would be one more page that I would tear into tiny pieces and drop in the trash can. In my frustration, I called my mom with tears rolling down my face.

"Mama, what am I going to do? I can't model or sew anymore, I can't help the girls with their lessons, and I can't learn this stupid braille!"

"Jean, who told you that you couldn't?" she asked.

"I've tried over and over again," I said.

"Put it away and try it again later. Don't worry; you'll learn to do it all. I know you will because you're not a quitter."

It was the first time I had cried to Mama since the day I had been diagnosed with my eye disease. I thought to myself, *I will never make Mama worry about my being blind again.* She had done everything possible for her children. She would always encourage us to shoot for the stars. She'd say, "Follow your dreams and always do whatever you choose to the best of your ability, and when you've done that, that's all you can do."

Do the best you can do. I repeated the words to myself a couple of times.

I heard Mama say, "Jean, are you alright? Do you want me to come over?"

"No, Mama, I'm fine. I just had to be reminded that some things don't come easy and I can't give up. It's getting late. I'll talk to you in the morning. Love you, Mama," I said as I hung up the kitchen phone.

I walked back to the dining room and put my hand on the braille writer. *You may be complicated, but I will figure you out. Tomorrow's another day.* I went quietly to my bedroom and put my arm across both girls. Just having them near made me feel blessed even in my darkest hours. The one thing I knew for sure was I couldn't give up.

***

I met lots of people at the center who were blind, and for the first time I felt no need to apologize to anyone because of my own blindness. Mrs. Louise was at the center every week. No matter what the weather was like, she would be there. She was so full of wisdom, each conversation seemed to nourish my spirit, and I felt a connection with her that was different from what I had with other people at the center. It was something I couldn't explain. Sometimes you just know when a person is genuine, and that influence helps to shape your life.

Mr. George was the first person I met in the craft class. He was an older man who had the energy of a twenty-year-old. He had very limited vision, but he tried so hard to focus with what little sight he had. He loved making leather crafts and managed to talk me into having a class at my house for a few months. He insisted that one day a week just was not enough time, and four others agreed with him.

I had convinced myself that all I wanted to do was get out of the house. I thought I wasn't interested in making friends, but that was a lie, and after spending time with these people, I had to admit the truth: I cared about them and what was going on in their lives. I wanted to help each one of them make the life they were living better, and in doing so I made mine better to. I didn't have to leave my cane at home because someone else felt uncomfortable anymore. I wanted to know just how naysayers thought I felt when I had a bruised thigh from bumping the corner of a table, or when they forgot to tell me about the curb ahead of me that I had missed as I stumbled into the street, or when people were talking about me in a whisper or talking to me as though I were deaf. I had been a model before the blindness, and now all my dreams were gone. I could no longer pursue my career, I had to come to grips with the fact that my life would never be the same. The beauty of seeing my daughters' features as they grew up or watching as they participated in activities, their graduations, and even their weddings had been stripped from my view.

My babies were so young; how could I have a normal life with them ,and how could this be fair? I often wondered what I could do to make this journey a smoother one, one from which I would have memories like other parents to hold on to for the rest of my life. I wanted to be angry, but I didn't know who to be angry with. Retinitis pigmentosa (RP) had stripped me of my vision, and all I had left was a gray that did an excellent job of blocking out everything.

I wanted to learn new things and participate in activities. I wanted my dignity back. I was the one made to feel different, as if I just didn't fit in. Even among family and most friends, I felt out of place, almost as if there were a room full of strangers talking all around me but not to me. I knew their voices but often wondered what their facial expressions were like when they were talking to me. It was as if they were holding their breath when I got up to move across the room; all conversations stopped and started again when I reached even the shortest distance. All that was missing was the sound of their applause for every little action I made. How many times had I done that same thing when I had sight? There was no doubt in my mind that they hadn't given my abilities any thought at all, and now my disability was driving them crazy.

My family and I went to church almost every Sunday, and I had no doubt in my mind about God's love for me. My mother had always told us that some things happen in life just to make you stronger. That all sounds good, but I found myself searching for yet one more answer from God. *Just how much strength do I need, Lord, and why me?*

A friend of Mama's invited us to her church one evening because she knew I had been having problems with my sight, and she was not going to take no for an answer. One or both of us was going to be at that Thursday evening service, so I told Mama that she didn't have to go and that I would join her friend instead.

To my surprise, the minister called me up to the front of the church for prayer. I walked up the center aisle, stopped, and immediately someone grabbed my arm. I felt a hand smack my forehead, and oil began to run down my face. I knew who it was then; it was the minister. He had one hand on the back of my head, and the other had oil on it. He was saying a prayer. Instinctively his hand smacked the oil on me, almost making me lose my balance. I was leaning backwards each time he smacked me with his hand. I felt confused at this point. *Why won't Ms. Bertha come and get me out of here? He's saying that I've lost my sight because someone sinned.*

"This blindness is the work of the devil," he proclaimed, "and I need you to ask for forgiveness!"

I asked God to forgive me, but I didn't know for what. I didn't know if my parents had sinned or that evil had anything to do with my loss of sight. I just remember praying to myself, *Please, Jesus, let your will be done, and get this man away from me.*

The ride home was very quiet, and when Mama came to the door, she took one look at me and asked, "What happened to you?"

Mama could read our expressions very well, and I'm sure that with all the mixed emotions I was feeling, she had to know something was wrong. I told her that she no longer had to pray for me because I'd already asked for forgiveness for everything, including things I hadn't even done. The next morning, we had a good laugh about it, although I admitted, all jokes aside, that I would never go back there again. Those people scared me half to death.

Lisa was only five when I lost my vision, and I told Ron how I tried to remain as active as possible in her life. I often sat in her classroom observing the activities and lesson plans, but most of all I wanted her to know I was there for her. Her teachers got to know me very well, and so did her classmates. I was selected as the volunteer parent of the year, which made my child very happy. During an assembly, they gifted me with a certificate, and as we went to the front of the entire school to receive it, Lisa told me that I was the best mom. I gave her a great big hug and wished with all my heart that I would one day see my child again.

It was a very short walk to the school, so most days I would stand in the yard while Lisa walked from the middle of the block to the corner where she met up with her friends, and they crossed the street together and walked the other half a block. I had walked the path to the school many times during the summer with her, and as I timed in my mind how long it would take her, I thought, *She should be at the left turn now. This walkway will take her straight to the classroom door.* I couldn't see her, but as usual, before she left home I told her how pretty she was with her really deep dimples and beautiful hair.

Several years had passed since then, and I was trying to hold on to every little detail that identified my child: her smile, the color of her eyes, and how they would change based on the color of her clothes—memories that were so special. I felt a tear roll down my face as I thanked God for my children.

Latrice was no longer an arm baby, but Lisa loved being a big sister from the very beginning! Whenever I sat on the sofa to give Latrice a bottle, Lisa would sit down beside me so she could hold it. She often helped me fold the diapers and match up the socks for both of them, and when she wasn't bursting with energy that only outdoors could contain, she would play with her little sister while I got some ironing done for the next week. I often thought, *Lisa is so young. . . . Am I asking too much of her?* I thought maybe I should wait for an adult or my teenage sister to come over, but Lisa would sit at the table with me, reading off the amount due for the phone and utility bills.

"Latrice, watch so one day you can help me and Mama get the bills ready to be mailed. Right, Mama?" Lisa stated.

"Lisa, do I get to put the stamps on this time?" Latrice asked. "Mama, will you give me a job too?"

"Yes, you may," I said, answering Latrice, who was always so eager to help. "You girls are awesome, and thank you for being my little helpers!"

When Latrice was born, I held her in my arms and traced her lips, nose, and eyes gently with my fingertips. I prayed that God would give me an image of my child that I could hold onto for life.

Mama had sat on the sofa beside me and said to me, "She is adorable, Jean, with her almond-shaped eyes, her thin lips, and keen nose just like your aunt Dora. My grandbabies are beautiful, and even if you can't see her, what a blessing your two little girls are."

"I know, Mama. I wish I could have seen her just once," I said quietly as I rubbed the back of her tiny hand. The doctors had told me I would be about sixty before my sight was gone except for light perception. I gave birth to Latrice when I was twenty-three and was not able to see her features at all. I smiled as I fought to hold back the tears. "Mama, do you want to hold your grandbaby?"

She took her in her arms. "She is so tiny and precious." I remember how we spent the next couple of hours handing her from one person to the next as she took little catnaps.

I would protect and love my daughters with all my heart and pray each day that God would be with them, just as Mama had prayed for us. I knew my girls would be blessed.

Summers were the most fun when the girls couldn't wait to finish breakfast to go out to play on their swing set and sliding board in the backyard. They enjoyed having their aunt Bae, cousins, or friends over, and I would listen to them play from the dining room or kitchen window. Whenever they didn't want to play at home, we walked the short distance to the school playground, where we always had a good time. They followed instructions really well and knew all the rules: "Never talk to a stranger or go anywhere with a stranger, never take anything to eat from a stranger, and never go so far away that I can't hear you."

It was a joy to play on the monkey bars, the sliding board, and the swings with my children. Lisa pointed out to me one day that the chains on the swings were much longer than the ones at home, and if we tried really hard, our feet could probably touch the sky. With both my girls on either side of me, it was then that I realized it doesn't matter where you are in this world as long as love surrounds you.

***

"Hey, Mama, I was thinking of something that all three of the girls might enjoy!"

I called to find out what it would cost for the girls to take karate lessons, and the sensei was so nice. He said it would be a pleasure to have them and for me not to worry about the cost, that he would work out a payment plan for me that I could afford. I said to Mama, "So if you are willing to drive us there, I can take care of the cost, and the girls can whip some butt whenever necessary!"

I karate-chopped the mattress, and Mama laughed. "Girl, stop before you break your hand."

"We can take a look at the school this week if you want," I explained. "He also said we could hang out there to watch the kids in one of the classes before we sign them up."

"Do you think Latrice is old enough to do that?" Mama asked. "She's so small, I don't want to see her get hurt."

"There are some girls there her age, Mama, and if she can't handle it, the sensei will let me know. It's a very constructive activity that teaches self-discipline and respect for others. If someone wants to start a fight with them, it will make the girls stop and think, *Is this how I need to handle this situation? Maybe it would be wise to walk away instead of fighting.* I'm sure the sensei doesn't want to create a bunch of pint-size bullies but rather people who can respect the illustrative art form taught in karate."

Chapter 3

Sunshiny Days

Ron called and said he had gotten a ride to come over. It was his brother, Preston, who they called Moochie, that would be bringing him. I thought I heard a car stop in front of the house, so I went out the side door and walked toward the curve. I called out Ron's name just as he was closing the car door.

"Hey, Jean, let me introduce you to my brother," Ron said.

"Hello, it's nice to meet you," I said, and his brother replied in kind.

"It's a beautiful sunny day!" his brother exclaimed, and we both agreed. Moochie continued his declarations. "No, I mean it's a beautiful day. It's a beautiful sunshiny day!"

I had no idea what was going on with him, but I thought he was either a strange guy or he wanted to be a weatherman. We bid him goodbye and made our way back into the house.

I inquired about his brother's odd nickname, and Ron replied that it was just one of those nicknames that didn't make sense but stuck. "Once you get to know him, you'll like him," Ron said.

I agreed with him, adding, "You know, one day you will have to meet my other sister, Dora, and her children."

My sister and I had always had a very close relationship no matter how far apart we were. We had enough love for each other to close the distance between us. There was no way a guy could be dating me and not meet my big sister.

We settled in on the sofa and passed the time talking for what felt like hours. Ron told me that he was a graduate of Ball State University, where he had received a bachelor's degree in health science and counseling. I knew now why he was such an attentive listener and why I was so at ease talking to him. He had moved from Indiana to Washington and had lived in Texas for a while before he came back to Indiana, where we met.

Well, I guess that explained why he was so good with the long white cane. He wasn't afraid to leave home and go out on his own. He thought he could do it without sight. It was his curiosity that overpowered his feelings of fear and made him ambitious enough to reach his goals.

"Jean," he said, "I had a really hard time getting work when I first graduated from college. I got turned down for so many positions until sometimes I felt like giving up. I did some jobs as a volunteer and later got hired full time. The pay wasn't what I always expected, but it was better than nothing. I knew I was qualified and capable of doing any of the jobs I had applied for, but all they saw was a blind man. They saw my disability, not my abilities."

"That's too bad," I sympathized.

Ron paused for a moment and agreed. "Yeah, it is, but I know I just can't give up. I've made some mistakes in life, but I've made some changes since I was a teenager, and my life's going to be better now."

We sat there on the sofa. Ron put his arm around me and held me close for a few minutes in silence, as if he were deep in thought. *No, I won't ask what he's thinking; I'll just let him share what he wants to with me in his own time*, I thought to myself.

Eventually I spoke. "Ron, everybody makes mistakes. You just have to ask for forgiveness and move past them," I said as I got up from the sofa. "The girls will be coming home soon. We're having a pot of chili. Would you like to have dinner with us?"

"Yes, I would, and thank you for asking." I could feel him smiling. "Is that chili from a can, or is it real homemade?"

I laughed. "Just know that if it's coming from my kitchen, it's homemade," I replied with a smile.

"Then baby, bring it on"

You're in for a treat, I thought. Everyone always said my chili was excellent, so I was almost sure he would enjoy it too. Ron watched television while I was cooking when he heard the doorbell ring.

It was the girls coming home, finally. They gave me the usual hug and kiss and jumped into explaining about the fun they'd had with their dad. "Mama, we had so much fun at Daddy's. He took us skating, and we played with some fun games. Oh, Mama, is that chili in the pot? Can we eat now?"

Before I could answer them, they heard Ron's voice. "Who wants to play a game?" They ran to the living room screaming with excitement.

"I'll divide the money for all four of us," Lisa said as she started to make four stacks of each denomination.

Ron enjoyed playing with the girls and was on the floor by the time they got the Monopoly board and dice out to play. I had no idea what was going on when I heard the girls making a blowing sound, so I went to the doorway and asked. "What are you three up to?" As I came closer, I found both girls on their knees, posed in positions to roll the dice.

"They're my good luck charms. I'm showing them how to roll craps," Ron replied easily. With a slightly puzzled look on my face, I said, "What are you talking about?"

He said with laughter, "Rolling dice, Jean. It's just as important to have street sense as it is to have book sense."

"Yeah, Mama, we'll blow on yours too, and you can roll them and say, 'Come on, lucky seven!'"

To my amazement, I heard Lisa exclaim, "Oh yeah, baby needs a new pair of shoes!"

Realizing then that I was looking from one kid to the other, they decided to keep silent. I took a pillow from the sofa and hit Ron's head with it. "They are little girls, and I hope they will grow up to act like young ladies. My girls don't need to know how to gamble, and neither do I. We'll finish the game later. Now, let's eat while the chili is hot."

Lisa helped Ron make all his moves on the board, and Latrice helped me land my lucky shoe on the right space. I thought to myself, *If I were a gambling woman, I would bet everything I own that the odds were in my favor and my girls are really happy.* I couldn't have asked for much more than that.

***

The seasons changed, and I watched Ron shovel the snow from our sidewalk while the girls played in the snow. I made the three of them hot chocolate to warm them up, and the four of us would snuggle in the living room and watch television. Then it was springtime, and Ron edged the lawn and cut the grass for me. He always said, "If you can walk a straight line, you can cut a straight line."

My mom thought his cutting skills were as good as any sighted person's, and he had no problem making her lawn look just as nice. "You know, I think he really likes you," Mama said in a low whisper.

I glanced at Mama and smiled. "I certainly hope so," I whispered as I turned to go back in the house.

The Wednesday visits that got Ron and me from the center to my house were nice and gave me a chance to get to know him better. But he wanted to see me more often, and need I add, it was perfectly alright with me! My aunt Lee always had dinner ready when I came home from the center, and it was Ron's luck that she loved to cook some of her favorite meals for him. Men always say, "The way to a man's heart is through his stomach." Ron was tall and thin, but his appetite never called for small servings, and it always made us laugh when Latrice would try to eat the same amount of food Ron ate. She was tiny but very competitive. The amount of food she ate was unbelievable. Even I had to frown at the large portions she wanted on her plate.

After watching how much Lisa and I were eating, Latrice decided, "I'm a girl, and girls don't eat as much as boys."

Good looks, charm, and money couldn't get you a date with me if my daughters didn't like having you around. The way to this mother's heart was to respect and care for all three of us. I guess you could say it was a package deal that always included them. Ron lucked up because they adored him and would ask him, "Please stay over here with us, Mr. Ron."

I responded, "He just may be able to stay tonight, especially if it keeps snowing like this." God must have been on Ron's side that night, I thought to myself. There was a snowstorm, and sure enough, Ron had to stay over because he didn't have a ride home. It was a Kodak moment.

There he was . . . six-foot two-inches sleeping in a twin canopy bed. *Yeah, he must like me a lot.* I smiled to myself and sat down on the rug at the side of the bed to finish our conversation before he fell asleep.

Lisa and Latrice shared a bedroom, which was now used only for getting dressed and storing their belongings. Ever since the divorce, they had slept in my bed, so they thought it was a great idea to give up their room for Mr. Ron.

"I know you're wondering why you are in here and they are in my bed, but you need to understand that I'll always give my girls respect, and when they're grown up, they'll respect me too," I said to him. "If we are meant to be together, it will happen at just the right time. Until then, let's enjoy this friendship we're developing."

He nodded in understanding and commented on how I was a good mother. On that note, I got up from the soft white rug. "Thank you for being so understanding. Good night, Ron. I'll see you in the morning," I said as I flicked the light switch off and quietly eased into my bed with my daughters, trying not to disturb either one of them.

***

At the Center, Ron would challenge me to get more involved in the blind community. The people who were blind at the center wanted to start a support group for the blind members and their spouses that gave us an opportunity to discuss our feelings concerning our blindness. I was amazed to see how difficult it was for some to deal with their loss of sight, while others had family members who wanted to treat them as if they were helpless.

Ron would say to us, "They are only doing them a disservice, and what will happen to them when they are all alone?"

I certainly didn't have all the answers, but I was sure of one thing: the only thing that made me different from anyone else was my blindness, and if I learned how to do things differently, I could make the adjustments necessary to tackle the task that would arise.

Ron went on to say, "People who are sighted want to treat people who are blind like they are deaf. One would think that our hearing is bad, but that is not the case, so there is no need to yell. We are adults too, so why do some sighted people feel it is necessary to talk down to us?"

Ron and Paul, another member at the center, seemed to not only have valid questions, but they also had answers. They were excellent mentors and seemed to have a different perspective than most blind people I had met.

In the group discussion, Ron said to us, "There is no need to insult my intelligence by talking down to me, and there is no need to treat me like I'm helpless just because I can't see. There is one thing we need to impress on others, and that is we are no different from any other normal person. There is nothing wrong with our minds. We just can't see. Don't let the use of this long white cane fool you. I put my pants on the same way a sighted man does, one leg at a time."

My attention went from Ron to Paul, who was sitting at the end of the long banquet table. Paul cleared his throat and said, "There are certain skills that are required for you to become an independent blind person. And you cannot let anyone or anything stop you. No matter how difficult it is, learning your braille skills will give you the ability to read books, magazines, and other printed materials. Learn to use your cane. It's not embarrassing to carry it if you learn to use it properly. If you need help, don't be ashamed to ask for it." He cleared his throat again and continued saying, "We can do this together. None of us have all the answers, but we will do the research and help you reach your goals. But we have to stand together."

Chapter 4

Life As It Is . . .

RON

I lay in my bed with a million thoughts running through my head. I tried to shut them out, but a voice in my head said, "I need you to reflect on your life, and then you can move on." I'm only seventeen, and I should have so many years ahead of me. I know in life there are no guarantees; there is only the here and now and a hope for tomorrow. Dear God, please hear my prayers for tomorrow!

I was the oldest son with seven other siblings, and we were a handful for our parents, each new birth giving them one more mouth to feed. But ever since I was a young boy, my mother went to church. She surely believed that God would provide, and so He did. Myra and Marzette Brown shared many experiences that kept them together through the good and bad times, but as with most black families, our mother was holding onto something inside of her that gave her strength to endure, the kind of strength that lets you know deep down inside that you can make it no matter what the situation is, that you could weather the storm and come out stronger on the other side.

Like every other kid, I played hard, and my passion was sports. I was good in basketball, and every chance I got to play, I was on the court. Maurice and Lorenzo were my two best friends, and they had a love for sports too. I thought about that for a few minutes, and then my mind went racing on to something else. Getting an education was important in our house, and I thought about what my trade would be. I was going to go into the refrigeration and cooling business with my cousin, and I would be able to manage just fine. I had a girlfriend, and I knew that one day if we continued to date, I would marry her, buy a cozy little house, and raise a family. But that wasn't in the plans just yet.

I was a popular young man in school. My future looked pretty clear to me, so I wasn't going to make any unnecessary changes. I would commit to someone one day, but for right now, I was enjoying my life without strings attached. I shook my head slowly and thought to myself, "Just stop thinking," but I couldn't. As a little boy, I used to sit on the front steps of our house and read a book that I love titled *Follow My Leader*. I was so fascinated with the story that I read it all the time to anyone who would listen. Then I remembered dreaming about my friends and my being in a basement. Then they would all leave together. I would be in the basement alone, walking in a circle with outstretched arms, crying out to my friends for help. It was a nightmare, and periodically it would return to frighten me once again. I would wake up in a cold sweat and turn on the light in my room just to make sure it was really a dream.

Jean said that we live our lives hoping we don't make the wrong decisions because we all know that there are consequences to face for every action we take. I always knew that life was about standing up for what you believed in, having fun, experiencing new things, and taking chances when the rest of the world took precautions. It's funny how you think you are invincible until something or someone proves you wrong.

I had a woodshop class the last hour of the day, and when the bell rang, I went to the locker and put everything away for the day. There was a poster of a boy playing, which had very vivid colors and read, "This is what you see." The oblong poster was divided in half, and the other side of it was black with white letters that read, "This is what a blind person sees." I heard the bell ringing, but I stood there looking from one side of the poster to the other side. The caption at the bottom read in bold letters, "So wear your safety goggles."

Everything happens for a reason. I know this is true, so I kept telling myself, "There has to be a reason why, why I'm in total darkness now." I was taking a shorter route home, laughing and talking with my friends, when suddenly I saw a flash of light, and I felt as if I were being stung by thousands of bees.

I had been shot in the face with a shotgun.

I started running, as if that would stop the stinging sensations that were covering my face, chest, and back. The shock to my body was so great that I collapsed to the ground and lay there screaming for help. I could hear voices around me. "I'll go get Mama," said Preston.

Moochie's voice was filled with an urgency that told my mother something was very wrong, that this was no joke nor a lie. "Come on, Mama, it's Ronnie. He's been shot!" My mother ran to the house four doors down where they had carried me. When she saw her child, her knees started to buckle. I heard someone say, "No, Myra, you can't do that. You've got to be strong." It felt as if the hands of time had stopped. I was crying out in pain, lying on the floor for what seemed like an hour, although it was only a few minutes until the ambulance came. They performed emergency surgery, and that was when I felt as if time had stood still.

Doctor Roberts entered the room with an expression on his face that I couldn't read. He introduced himself to my mother. I knew I needed to be strong, but I was too weak to protest.

My mother sat back down on the cushioned seat and asked him, "Will he be alright?"

The doctor looked away from her for a second to check his notes, and then his eyes met hers again. He said, "There are some pieces of the pellets we couldn't remove, but over a period of time, some will work their way out of his skin. He's lost a great deal of blood, and there is a lot of swelling." The doctor clicked the button on the top of his pen and continued, saying, "I wish there were more I could do for him, but we will try to keep him as comfortable as possible."

The doctor was not optimistic at all. He said, "Your son has made it out of surgery, but if he lives, he will be a vegetable. Mrs. Brown, there was too much damage to the optic nerves to save any of his sight. I'm sorry."

I heard my mother crying out to God to give me another chance. Not knowing what had happened or why, she prayed for the life of her child. Bandages covered my entire swollen face except my mouth. The doctor had put in a trach for me to breathe. If I wanted to say anything, I was given a pen to write with and a tablet. I was heavily sedated, so most of the time I was asleep. My mother thanked God for His mercy and grace. I knew that it was because of His love that I would live. My mother didn't know what my condition would be, but she knew she would take care of me, and God would prepare me for whatever was going to be on the road ahead.

It felt as if I had been hospitalized for a long time, but it had only been a couple of weeks. In an instant I had gone from twenty-twenty vision to none. I had so many questions, I didn't know where to start. At night when the house was quiet, I heard no footsteps or laughter. There was nothing but silence and this dreaded darkness, so I would listen to the television or a book on tape until I fell asleep. It had to be the wrath of God. I must have made Him really angry at me for Him to let this happen. I would pray, "Lord, I'm sorry. Please forgive me. I was in too much pain when I got shot to ask, but I'll never take my life or your love for granted anymore."

My mother didn't let me lie around and feel sorry for myself for too long. She was a strong woman, and she was not going to enable me, so she called my best friend, Maurice, and asked if he still had his tuxedo cane. When he told her that he did, she asked for him to bring it over. When he arrived, my mother called me to the living room.

"Ron, I don't know a lot about how blind people do things, but you have to go to school. I want you to use this tuxedo cane, and if you get lost, just stop and ask for assistance. I'll help you all I can," she said. "But you can't give up now. Some things will seem very difficult for you at first, but don't worry; you'll get through it, son."

I didn't know what to say, but just as she wanted to alleviate my fears, I desperately wanted to do the same for her.

"I'll be alright, Mother; you'll see. They'll call me Mr. Cool."

She stepped to the side of the coffee table and said, "Alright then, Mr. Cool."

I could tell by the tone of her voice that I had cheered her up, and that was all that mattered. As I went down the stairs to my room, I thought to myself, "What a way to get a pretty girl to help me. 'I don't know which way my classroom is; can you walk there with me?' Being blind won't be all bad," I thought. "I'll just make it work in my favor."

Our mother helped me complete most of my assignments, and I graduated with the senior class. I could never repay her for all she did for me. As difficult as it was for her, she became my mobility instructor and my reader for all my classes. My mother was determined to get me through school, and even though I knew it would be a challenge, I had to make it happen.

I heard Ron's story, and it tore at every fiber of my heart. He was just a kid, a young boy who was about to enter manhood without his sight. The graphic details of the damage done by the shotgun made me feel ill, and I thought to myself, *What a shame that he now has to carry the fragments of that day with him always.* I heard the cry in the strength of his voice. I knew that the boy in him still didn't understand the answers to all the questions he was seeking. Somehow I knew the search for answers would go on for years to come.

I don't know whose idea it was to start an affiliate of the National Federation of the Blind in Northwest Indiana, but Paul Howard was president and Ron Brown served as his vice president. Paul was determined to talk me into joining this organization of blind people, so he came to my house to convince me there was work to be done in the blind community. He said, "Think about your strengths and your weaknesses. Isn't there something you want to offer that will help build our chapter?"

"I'm pretty good at raising funds," I said.

"Good! We will need a fundraiser in order to support our affiliate," he exclaimed. "Our first meeting will be next month. The meetings will be held at the library downtown on the second Saturday of each month. I think we'll start at ten o'clock so we can finish up around noon. So we'll see you there!" Paul said with some excitement in his voice.

This guy reminded me of Marlon Brando in the movie *The Godfather*. He had a low, hoarse-sounding voice that made me think that at any given moment, he was going to say to me, "I'll make you an offer you can't refuse."

The phone rang just as we were wrapping up our conversation. When I answered, Ron was not surprised when I told him that it was Paul, so I knew it had been a well-planned visit engineered by the two of them.

"Are you going to join our new chapter?" Paul asked.

"Yes I am, and I'm going to chair fundraising,"

"That sounds like a plan," he said. "I'll talk to you later about it, and you can bounce some ideas off me if you like." We agreed and said our goodbyes.

Ron and Paul had joined the organization while they were students at Ball State, when NFB state president Marc Maurer and his wife, Patricia, were visiting so they could recruit students from the university to strengthen the student division. Yes, Ron and Paul were eager to join the federation but for all the wrong reasons. President Maurer had boxes of candy for them to sell, and they ate it. President Maurer was serious about the struggles that blind people had to fight. Ron and Paul saw girls, girls, and more girls. They knew this was an opportunity they couldn't resist. The two of them were all for having a good time. They knew very little about the organization, but they would learn all that stuff later. There was plenty of time to learn how to be a dedicated member. For now the focus was on having fun.

The two of them had finished high school together. Paul became Ron's mentor during their senior year. Being blind was new to Ron, who had lost his sight at age seventeen. However, Paul, who had been blind since he was five, had been well educated in blindness skills. Ron went away for the summer before college and learned grade one and two braille that summer. He would still need a reader and a tape recorder, but he would make it through school without some of the difficulties he had to deal with his senior year. He was fascinated with his new way of reading and all that set him apart from everyone else.

Ron said, "I didn't think I was better because I was blind, and it didn't make me happy that I had lost my sight. But I wanted to learn everything I could so people wouldn't look at me and think I was less than they were or that I didn't have the ability to learn because of my blindness." Ron went on, saying, "Jean, when I first lost my sight, I would lie in my bed at home and think about the changes I would need to make in my life. I knew everything was going to be different now. I'm black and I'm blind; I'd better get busy." That was when I got serious about school and life in general. I hadn't done everything right, but I was trying to make some changes for the better. Belonging to this organization has helped me tremendously. Just wait until you decide what you want to do; you'll see what I mean.

Our chapter was small in the beginning, but each member got involved in the fundraising projects, the march on Washington, and the community outreach projects, and we developed a strong support system for our membership. It took me by surprise when Mama and Aunt Lee became members. They always had discussions with me about the topics held at the meeting, often admitting how shocked they were at the discrimination we had to fight just because of our blindness.

"This is not the eighteen-hundreds!" Mama said to us on the way home from a meeting. "Why do people think you should be content with a rocking chair and a radio in a closed-up room? Those days are long gone! People who are blind should be treated the same as sighted people. How do you degrade a person because of a disability?" Mama was absolutely right. The question in my mind was, What could we do to change this very obvious injustice? I don't know that the National Federation of the Blind is the solution to all the issues we have to face, but I do know that I would rather be a part of this organization than fight alone for my rights.

Our first fundraiser would be starting that week with 150 tin cans of turtle candy now stacked in my basement. I looked at the cases of candy and thought, *You'd better start calling everyone you know to pull this one off.*

Mamie and Laura were the first to say, "Girl, bring us a case. We can get that candy sold in no time." So the project was off to a good start, and almost every call gave us another sale.

Filled with excitement after the last call, I exclaimed, "Yeah, let's keep those turtles moving! Ron and Paul had wanted a fundraiser, and they got their wish. Now let's see how eager they're going to be to sell this candy."

Chapter 5

The Right Tools

I attended my first national convention and heard Dr. Kenneth Jernigan, our national president, and I was in awe! I had never heard a blind person deliver a speech, but when the gabble went down, the voice that filled the room was a powerful one, welcoming a room of about three thousand people. I was never more impressed. The convention week was filled with meeting after meeting, and each one gave me more knowledge and enthusiasm than before. I had never heard a sighted person deliver a speech with more eloquence than he had just done.

Ron tapped my arm and asked quietly, "You do know that he is reading braille, don't you?"

"No," I whispered in amazement, "I did not know that." I could not imagine anyone reading with such speed and accuracy with his fingers. I learned something that day that I hope to never forget, and that is blind people can do whatever they want, if they are given the training, the proper tools, and the opportunity. There were people from every state in that room. Some were sighted, but the majority were totally blind or visually impaired. They were from all walks of life, and the fact that they were blind didn't matter. They had their canes or their dogs to get them safely from one place to another, stopping and asking questions along the way.

I told Ron, "This is a new experience for me, and I am afraid to walk around this big hotel alone,"

"You don't have to worry, Jean. You are never lost, just displaced, so all you need to do is ask for directions." He had reduced his blindness to its lowest denominator. It was not a big deal in his mind, so he could not and would not let it be an excuse for not meeting the requirements needed to move forward.

I realized how strong a blind individual had to be to face the multitude of challenges in life. If success were to be accomplished, what would the steps be that got you there, and would you only try to succeed and fail? I didn't know what was expected of blind people, but I knew it was not the same thing that was expected of sighted people. I had heard in so many ways the call for justice and equality for all people. Although removed many years ago, I realized that the chains that held the wrists and legs of brothers and sisters buried beneath the ground we walk upon, the ones that were tossed into the waters to rust, still exist, but they can no longer hold a strong man down. These are the invisible chains that recognize no religion, race, creed, or color but take offense at the long white cane. How could an employer deny employment to someone qualified because he or she carries a cane? How does our court system remove a child from the care of its mother because of her blindness? Is there a point when daylight meets darkness and trades in ignorance for knowledge, when you can replace unjust actions and verbal manipulations for dignity and respect for our fellow man? I know what the battle is all about, and without a doubt it won't be a bloody mess, but it will be a verbal lashing that will be felt throughout this nation for years to come. I had been inspired by a man who was knowledgeable and powerful. He was our leader, and he had convinced me that one day we would not be treated as second-class citizens.

I thought back to the day I became a member of this organization. There was doubt and uncertainty in both my heart and my mind that no longer exist. Yes, indeed, our equality is worth fighting for.

***

I finally met Ron's immediate family: Myra, his mother, and his dad, Marzette. There were five sisters and two brothers. One was in the military but would be coming home soon. It was Labor Day, and they were having a family cookout. The aroma that filled the house was to die for. Two of Ron's aunts were seated at the dining room table when I came in with Ron and Moochie. I had brought my daughters with me, and all of his sisters wanted to meet them and the new girl their brother had been dating.

Ron introduced us to his family, and just when I thought I had met the last person, I heard more people coming in from the back door. I wondered if Ron would have been this nervous if we had shown up for Thanksgiving dinner. I smiled and said hello to everyone. I stood my cane against the wall close to the arm of the sofa and sat down.

I listened as Ron's mother moved swiftly from one room to the other. She finally stopped at me and asked, "Would you like me to make you a plate?"

"Yes, please," I answered, adding, "Everything smells so good."

"Thank you. All the kids and Ron are on the back porch. Do you want to go out there?"

I told her I would, and her hand touched mine as I stood. "I'll show you to a seat. The porch is enclosed, and if you want to come back in, it's just right through the kitchen. Here's the doorway. There's a seat next to Ron," she said as she pulled it out a little for me.

The girls all snickered again at whatever they were talking about before I entered the room. Margret was the oldest. She was married with two children of her own, and although she was no longer at home, Carmen, Trina, Toni, and Stephanie (known as Miss Ann) were still at home and in school. The two brothers, Preston and Darryl, were a part of the first set of children and were on their own now. The house was filled with a real sense of family. Some of the cousins were there as well, which added up to a house full of happiness, jokes, little ones crying, adults who kept everything under control, and Miss Ann, the youngest sister, who kept everyone in check at the ripe old age of ten.

Later on, when it was time to go home, I told Ron how I felt.

"The girls had a good time, Ron, and so did I. Being with your family was cool. They are so down to earth."

"Yeah, my dad really likes you," Ron said. "He thinks I've got good taste in women."

"Is that right?" I asked playfully as I slipped both arms around his waist to hug him.

"I think that you are the girl for me and that God answered my prayer," Ron said, hugging me tightly.

"And what exactly did you pray for?" I asked.

"I prayed that God would send the perfect girl for me, and here you are," he said softly.

It was a moment I'll never forget, and his words made me want to hold him even longer.

"Ma-ma!" Both Lisa and Latrice were calling me with all the lung power they had. I heard footsteps coming up the stairs as quickly as possible, and both girls, as if they were rehearsing for a synchronized part in a commercial, again said, "Mama! Can we have some McDonald's? Please, Mama?"

"Well, we could if I had a way to go and get it," I said. They both let out a long sigh and turned to go back to the basement. "I'm sorry, girls," I said, "but we can get McDonald's this weekend when Mama comes to take us to the mall."

Ron had sat through our talk in silence and finally said, "Lisa, if you'll get the phone for me, I think we can get those burgers, fries, and four shakes."

"Ron, who are you going to call that will come all the way over here?"

"If the girls want fast food every now and then, we just have to figure out a way to get it for them, and right now the solution is to call a cab."

His solution worked. We placed our order at the drive-through window and made it back home before the fries got cold.

The girls said, "Ron, that was fun. Can we do it again?"

We all laughed, and he replied, "Yes, we'll do it again one day."

***

It was the first week of December, and I wanted the year to end filled with nothing but happiness for my girls and Ron. It was our one-year anniversary, and I was determined to enjoy myself. I thought to myself, *I'm going to throw caution to the wind and live it up this weekend.*

Ron had asked me the previous night if I wanted to go out. "Do you think you can get a sitter for the girls?"

"I'm sure I can," I replied, but when I hung up the phone, I wondered how we were going to get to wherever we were going. *I wonder if we are going alone. This is crazy! What am I doing? There's no way two totally blind people need to be out on the town partying alone. But I won't dare tell him that. I'll just go and see how it turns out.* We had gone to card parties before and had a good time with some friends but not to a club.

While arranging for my mother to babysit for me, I asked her, "Mama, what if I get lost from him?"

"I don't think he's going to let you wander that far away from him."

Aunt Lee was over visiting Mama, and I heard her in the background saying, "If she gets lost, they'll get lost together, and we'll have to come searching for both of them. You would think that man could see when it comes to keeping his eyes on Jean."

Later that evening, back at home, as I was about to figure out what I would wear that night, Ron handed me a gift bag. The black dress he had bought for me was a perfect fit; it was long-sleeved with a straight-line cut across the collarbone and a wide belt that accented my waist. The dress was simply elegant and seemed to drape nicely across my hips as it flared at the bottom. To complete the look, Ron had bought red three-inch heels with lots of straps. The only jewelry I needed was my watch and a silver eighteen-inch necklace.

As soon as I stepped out of the room, he said, "Come here, girl. Let me see you." He checked me out from head to toe, saying, "I can't believe it all fits you just right. I hope you enjoy yourself tonight, Jean."

"Oh, Ron, I'm sure I will," I replied.

He had arranged for a taxi to pick us up, and it arrived right on time. At the club, while the live band was playing, we got on the dance floor and found out just how in sync we were with each other's moves. There was a candle on the table that had seats for only two. As we listened to the music and talked, I knew there was no reason to hold onto any of the past that troubled me or made me have insecure feelings. But I couldn't help but think, *What if I open up to this man and he walks out of my life? I don't think I'm ready to deal with that. Well, for now I'll just enjoy him holding me tight and gliding across the dance floor as if we had practiced every dance and were the only couple on the floor.* I loved to dance, and I was enjoying every step with this tall, handsome, and good-smelling man. Yes, yes, yes, I could relive this night over and over again. "Swept for You Baby!" replayed itself in my head all night. It was an old song, but it had a brand-new meaning for me.

***

Mama and I went out to get a live Christmas tree with the help of Bae, Lisa, and Latrice. We pulled up to the lot as if the five of us knew exactly what we were looking for; we wanted nothing less than the best tree on the lot. It was the beginning of what could have been a Lucille Ball show. The tree trunk was too big for the stand, and I had no idea what I needed to do to make it fit. I was determined to solve this problem on my own, so why not try a carving knife and see if that would make the base fit? I chipped away at the tree, thinking to myself, *This may as well be an old oak tree that I'm trying to cut down from the yard.* I knew it wasn't as bad as all that, but I just wasn't getting anywhere, and my daughters were sitting on the floor watching me as if they knew it was hopeless.

After about an hour, I said, "Lisa, do you remember seeing the ax out in the garage?"

She was thrilled to be able to help and replied, "Mama, I can show you where it is!"

"Alright, the plan, my little one, is to put a board under the base of this old tree and take off a little at a time until the base is the right size for this stand."

"Okay, Mama, we'll help you!"

"I wish you could, but this is a job only Mama can do," I said. "But you two can help me decorate when the cutting is all done."

I had never seen anyone use an ax and hammer together, but this just had to work, I thought to myself. I was not going to disappoint my girls. I took the blade and placed it on the tree trunk, holding it still with my left hand at an angle. Here came the hard part, which was hammering the blade into the wood without making a total mess of our tree. I took the first chunk of wood off the base and went to work on the other side, pounding with all my might until what had been a round base was now a four-sided tree base. My hands were sore now, and my back felt as if I had worked in a field all day. No one would see it, and it had only three weeks to be in our house. "Lord, please don't let this tree fall." I said the words in a very low whisper, but I knew He heard each one.

Once it was in the stand lying on its side, I put on my jacket to prevent getting scratched up by all the branches. Giving the tree as much of a hug as I could stand, I stood it up, and the crowd of two cheered. Yes, I was their shero.

Lisa sat on the floor with lights all around her and made sure they were working. "If that's not enough lights," I said, "there are a few new packs in the closet." Latrice knew that her job would be to decorate the lower half of the tree, and I would take care of what she couldn't reach. After the garland had been put on the tree, I picked Latrice up to let her put the star on the top. As soon as it was in place, Lisa plugged in the lights. They were happy, and that was all that mattered to me.

I put both hands on my lower back and leaned from side to side and forward a few times to get some relief. I said, "Looks like I'm in need of a tub full of hot water with lots of bubbles and some Epsom salts for my aching muscles."

"Mama, when you finish, you can lay on the floor, and we can walk on your back. That will make it feel better."

"That sounds wonderful! Give me twenty minutes and I'm all yours."

The cold weather made me want a meal Mom had often made for Daddy when there was snow on the ground and the temperature was falling. She always said that in the winter, you need something that will stick to your ribs, so golden-brown chicken, ham hocks, pinto beans, and a skillet of hot corn bread would be our dinner today. I would call Delores as soon as the ham hocks and beans were ready because whenever that meal was cooked, there was one extra ham hock in the pot just for her.

I knew a lot of people, but my four best friends since high school were Dee, Jacqueline, Beverly, and Betty. It was strange how we didn't talk all the time, but whenever we did meet up, we picked up right where we'd left off and really enjoyed each other's company. I left a message for Delores, and I knew if she didn't come over that day, she would definitely be here the next. Ron would be over as soon as he could get a ride from the other side of town. Although Ron never complained about the effort he had to put into getting here, it was a job in itself. I knew the snow made our transportation issues worse, and there was nothing we could do about it.

I thought about making a bowl of potato salad to have with the leftover chicken later on that night. I knew now that as long as the meal included chicken, it would be alright with Ron. He said one day, "It does not matter how you cook it as long as there's some yardbird in the house. It can be fried, baked, broiled, boiled, or stewed. Just give me chicken!"

Some of the comments he made would make me laugh until I cried. "You are so silly," I would tell him, but once he got started, he was on a roll, from one subject to the next. His goal was to make me smile, and he always did.

Christmas Eve was always a special day for our family, and my girls were as excited as I was. We made Christmas-tree-shaped cakes to deliver to friends on our block. Once the white icing had been put on the cakes, the girls would decorate them with red, green, yellow, and blue colors that represented the little ball ornaments. We had decided to make a variety of cookies the previous year, but after finding the holiday cake pans, I knew they would not settle for anything else.

"Mama, let's make a yellow and a chocolate cake," Lisa said while Latrice wanted to make nothing but strawberry cakes. The girls usually agreed on most things, but this time it seemed that Lisa wanted to have her way because she was the oldest, and Latrice wanted to have her way because she was the baby.

"Girls," I said, "why don't we make all three of those flavors. And in case someone doesn't like those flavors, let's also make white cake!" Reaching that happy medium had us finished baking in no time.

Finishing up the baking early in the afternoon meant for me that I was right on schedule because the desserts had to be made for our dinner too. Mama, Bae, Dora, and her children, Demetrius, Lamont, and Lil, would all be coming over for a while to visit the next day. They were going to have dinner at their homes, but I always liked to have enough prepared in case someone wanted a plate while visiting or to take home for a snack.

"Put your coats on, girls. It's time to take the cakes," I said, and the girls ran to the closet to get their coats and boots on.

"Mama, which coat do you want?" Lisa asked.

"My gray jacket will be fine," I replied. "And my boots are at the door already. Thank you, sweetie."

The work was over, and now the fun would begin. I gave each girl a cake to hand to a neighbor, and then the three of us would say, "Merry Christmas, and have a happy holiday season!"

When we returned home, it would be a long night in the kitchen preparing the meal for Christmas Day, but my two little helpers were ready, or so they thought. The time flew by, and by eleven they were both asleep. I managed to tuck them both in with no questions. I was so pleased with the job I had done as Santa's helper getting them tired enough to fall asleep before midnight.

I picked up the phone to make a call. "Hello, Mama," I said as soon as she answered the phone. "I just wanted to check on you and Bae. Are you going to bed now?"

"Yes," she said. "I just turned my light off."

"Good. Then get some rest, and I'll call you in the morning. Love you, Mama."

"I love you too," she said.

I noticed how very tired she sounded. Mama loved holidays, but she always pushed herself the extra mile to make sure everything was as perfect as she could make it for us. I was certain that a holiday wouldn't have the same joy if she weren't here to share it with us. I hung the phone up on my little marble table beside my bed and prayed, *Lord, you know her needs. Please bless her spiritually, physically, and financially. Amen.*

I thought back to when Mama was diagnosed with bone cancer. The doctor had asked me to step into the waiting room so we could talk. He told me that there was no cure, but they could give her chemotherapy and radiation treatments. "It will make her feel sick sometimes, but if she keeps a positive attitude, it will help a lot," he said. "Jean, I want you to tell her because I think she will accept it a lot better if she hears it from you. This is how you can help your mother."

Tears rolled down my face, and without saying a word, the doctor placed a tissue in my hand. I dried my face, and he asked almost in a whisper, "Are you ready to go back in her room now?" I looked at him with what had to have looked like a blank stare, and he responded, "I'll be right here if you need me. Just go to the door and call me."

I set my purse on the chair a few feet from Mama's bed. "Are you sleep?" I asked her in a quiet voice.

"No, I'm still woke," she answered.

I went to the side of the bed and put one hand over hers. I held onto the bed rail with the other. The thought of what had to be said made me feel ill, but I knew I had no choice. *Oh God, I wish Dora and Arthur were at home with us. Bae is just a kid, and what if—?*

My thoughts were interrupted when Mama asked me what was wrong. I told her just what the doctor had said about her condition and quickly added, "But you'll be alright, Mama."

"I have two questions. The first is, Will you take care of Bae if something happens to me?"

"Mama, you know I will," I replied while holding back the tears that had formed in the wells of my eyes. I told her what I had always been told. "There is no failure in Christ, Mama, and by His stripes we are healed. You will be alright, Mama. We'll take care of you."

She had one more question. "Is all my hair going to fall out?"

"No, Mama!"

She replied, "That's what I've always heard."

"Well, Mama, if it does, I'll shave my head, and you and I will be wearing the sharpest wigs in town." That made her chuckle a little, but it made the tears I had tried so desperately to hold back come streaming down my face. "Don't ever worry, Mama. You will never go through anything alone. I'll be with you for every treatment and procedure you go through." I reached over the rail, and, giving her a gentle hug, I said, "I love you, Mama."

That was a few years before, and she'd been in remission for several years. I was just thankful for God's mercy and grace.

On Christmas Day, the girls woke me up, and they had obviously been up for a while. Lisa said, "Mama, I poured a bowl of cereal for us so you could sleep a little longer."

Both girls anxiously asked, "Can we open our presents now? Can we, Mama?"

"I'll get up right now," I said. "Merry Christmas! I love you two so much. Yes, let's open all the presents now!"

I spent the morning playing with the girls and cooking the rest of my dinner before the family arrived. The girls called their dad and his parents to wish them a merry Christmas. I knew they both missed him and that the feeling was the same for him. There was no doubt that he loved his girls and would do anything for them. The previous year right before Christmas, Lisa asked me if her dad was ever going to live with us again. I told her no, but that no matter where he was, he would always love her and her sister. I told her that it was our love that had changed, not his love for his daughters. I wondered if there was sadness or, even worse, anger behind those beautiful dimples, and I knew that only time would tell. Was she holding her feelings inside? Would they both grow up bitter towards me? If only I could have shielded them from this pain. I prayed the Lord would help us to be the parents they needed us to be.

I checked the time. "Oh, gosh! It's almost one o'clock! We need to get dressed before the doorbell starts ringing and you girls get caught in your pj's." There was something about the magic of this day that always made me feel like a kid as much as my daughters did.

Before long, family was arriving, and the house was full. "Merry Christmas, Jean," my sister called out as she entered the living room.

"Here I come," I said.

"You don't need to rush, Jean. Mama went to pick up Dora and the kids."

I said, "Well, come here, dear sister. I've got presents for you."

I was pleased that we all had such good relationships, we could talk about anything with each other. *That's how I want my girls to be, close, just like that,* I thought to myself.

Two cars pulled up one right behind the other, and the girls, still so filled with excitement, ran to the door once again, shouting that Grandma and Aunt Dora had arrived.

It wasn't long before all of the family and Ron had made it. All the gifts were opened that had been placed under the tree. The board games, dolls with their little outfits, and other toys were scattered all over the living room, which made it rather difficult to walk without stepping on something or someone, especially when they were all stretched across the floor playing the game Operation. I decided it was time for the children to give us some adult time, and so that we would not have to spoil their fun, they were sent to the basement. The kids all had something in common, which was that they all loved music, instruments, science, and reading, all of which they could do downstairs. What a joy to be able to give them their own space.

Hours later the house was almost quiet, and the girls were ready to change into their cozy pj's. "Anyone want cake and ice cream before bed?" I asked.

"I do, Mama!" they both yelled out from their bedroom.

"How about you, Ron? Would you like some too?" I asked as I went past his chair. I stopped, took two steps back, and leaned over to give him a kiss on the jaw.

He quickly said, "Yes, that sounds good, and I'll have some more of those kisses too."

With the sound of laughter in my voice, I replied, "I'd love to accommodate, but I'm rather busy."

The next day, the girls were gone with their dad, and I sat in the living room chair, lacing a leather wallet and thinking how blessed I was to have my daughters. They wouldn't be gone for long, but I missed them terribly.

I thought back on one particularly fond memory. Lisa, who wanted me to experience riding a bike, told me one day, "Get on behind me, Mama. Now, hold on," she said as we rode down the sidewalk. It was on that day she found out I had never ridden a bike, not even when I was sighted.

Latrice stayed on the front porch as I had asked her to and started clapping her hands when we reached the front yard, saying, "Mama, you rode the bike with Lisa!" She ran down the sidewalk to meet us.

Lisa said, "I'm going to tell Aunt Bae that I took you for a ride on my bike!"

Latrice said, "When I get bigger, I'll take you for a ride too, Mama!"

They were filled with excitement, but I had a feeling this would be my first and last time going for a joyride on a bike. I looked at them and said with a smile, "You do know that bike riding is not for everyone, don't you?"

When I was growing up, I would play volleyball in the backyard or baseball in the front yard with Arthur, Lovie, Prentice, and Malcom, but as soon as my white tennis shoes got dirty, playtime was over for me. Mama knew not to waste money buying a bike for me because it would have been parked in the garage collecting dust with all the other unused items.

Lisa had owned several bikes and was always willing to take her little sister for a ride. She said, "Mama, when Latrice gets older, I'll teach her to ride a bike like mine."

"Well, she couldn't have a better teacher." I smiled.

Chapter 6

Missing You!

"My flight will be leaving in the morning at seven, and I've got to get back home early so I can pack. One day you'll get a chance to go and check it out for yourself. Everyone will meet with the legislators from their own state to discuss the issues the national office has decided are the most important. Each state sends a group of people to represent their state. We are all given a fact sheet to learn so we are all on the same page," Ron explained.

"I understand," I said. I also understood Ron would be gone for a whole week, and I was going to miss him. I asked, "You will call while you're gone, won't you?"

"You know I will," he said as he gave me a really tight squeeze. "I'll call you when I get settled in my hotel room."

"I'll be right here waiting," I said.

The conversations were shorter but quite frequent because there were updates all during the day about the meetings and what the legislators chose to do with the information they had given to them.

"I miss you, Ron," I said, and he replied the same.

"Did you all do a good job at the bake sale?" Ron asked. "You know how important it is to raise funds, and every little bit helps."

"Yes, I do. The chapter members worked really hard to get everything donated, and some actually baked some of the cakes and pies themselves. I found out what an excellent cook Mamie and Lora are, and they hung in there with me to the very end of the day. They didn't leave until everything was sold. Pat made a couple of cakes that went really fast, and Aunt Lee made a peach pie that some guy paid thirty dollars for. Mrs. Dixon and Mama made cakes that they sliced into really large portions, and those were individually wrapped for sale. Our desserts sold like hotcakes! Ron, we had a ball today!"

"Well, you all did a good job," he said as he yawned. "We have to be on the Hill early in the morning, so I'm going to turn in now. I'll call you in the morning, sweetheart. I love you. Have a good night, and I'll talk to you whenever you can call."

The next day, the girls and I had plans to spend time with an acquaintance of mines.

"Make sure you put on warm sweaters. It's very cold out today, and I don't want either one of you to get sick." I yelled out to the girls.

"We will, Mama!" they both shouted.

"When we get to Ms. Cathy's house, are we still going to make pizza?" Lisa asked.

"I want to help make the pizza too, Mama," Latrice said.

I assured her that she would help. "It's got to be very difficult being the youngest in the group," I told her.

Cathy's girls, Lynn and Jennie, adored both Lisa and Latrice, so whenever they saw them, they were very attentive. Her daughters were teenagers, and I thought they were terrific girls with lots of talent and personality that would take them far in whatever careers they chose. They wanted to be rappers, and who wouldn't want two gorgeous girls entertaining them? In a few more months, they would be graduating from high school, and they would ask me, "Aunt Jean, will you come and see us if we make it big as rappers?"

"I'll be right there," I would say, "but it's not *if* you make it big; it's *when* you make it big! You two are beautiful and smart. You'll make it to the top in no time."

Lynn and Jennie were waiting for the girls to arrive so they could get our dinner ready.

"Come on, Lisa and Latrice. If we start now, it will be done when they get back from the bank."

"Hey, girls, wash your hands really good before you touch that food. I don't want to get cooties," I told them. The girls all ran to the sink. Each one of them was insisting that the other needed to wash a little longer.

"We'll be right back," Cathy said as we went out the back door to the alley where her car was parked.

I had learned to be more aware of sounds around me. Listening for what might have been dangerous for me or my girls was a way of life, and when I heard the car locks make their loud popping sound for the second time, I knew something was wrong.

"Cathy, did you take the lock off?" I asked.

"No, the doors are locked," she said as we continued to the bank. "Girl, we should stop and get gyros for dinner and let the girls eat pizza. There's a good place just a couple of blocks ahead. Do you want to stop?"

"No," I said. "The girls will be disappointed if we don't eat the pizza. Let's get gyros another day."

I felt the car coming to a slow stop and within seconds heard the back door open and then *slam!* I felt something very cold and hard being pressed against the back of my head and wondered if it was just a pipe. *Who is this, and what does he or she want?* I had pushed my purse off my lap to the floor and managed to get it under the seat most of the way, but it didn't matter. I knew now that it was a man, and he had made it clear that he would blow my f'ing brains out.

He applied as much pressure as possible to my head with the gun he held in his left hand. The first unexpected blow came to the right side of my head, and I leaned to the left. He grabbed a handful of my hair and pulled me back up. He reached over the seat with his right hand. He felt on the seat, checking the right side and then the left side. The stranger had made it clear that he was searching for something. Could he possibly have known that I had all this cash on me? There were more blows to the head, and with each I held my breath again. Why had I worn a dress that day? I felt him touching me, rubbing my legs, and then he was trying to push his hand farther up under my dress between my thighs. *Hold your breath and don't say a word to him*, I told myself, so in silence I thought, *Lord, help me.*

After rubbing my thighs, he moved his right hand to the front of the seat, reaching down to the floor of the car to pull up my purse, which he quickly tossed on the seat beside him. He was a man of few words, but the one he spoke planted a seed of fear in me that I had never experienced before in my life. He wrapped my hair around his hand to pull my head back up, only to hit me again. I could hear the contents of my purse being shaken out onto the seat. He took the envelope that contained all of our chapter's hard-earned money from the bake sale and four hundred dollars of my own money.

The man told Cathy, "Turn right here. Now, stop!" he yelled.

Cathy stopped and caused the car to jerk suddenly, but the man was getting out. Soon I could get help and see my babies. Cathy had done as she was instructed and never said a word. I thought that if we could get help, get someone's attention, maybe they could find this guy, and I could get our money back, but Cathy thought that was a crazy idea. "No, we should just get back to my house," she said.

Nothing about this felt right, and I knew I had to do something, so I began to blow her horn.

Cathy grabbed my hand and said, "What are you doing? What if he finds us?"

"I don't care. We've got to get some help!" I said as I pounded on her horn again.

"Well here come the police," she said in her cool and calm voice. The impression she gave me was one of frustration because I had just brought attention to our situation, and for some reason she didn't want that.

I could imagine the red light flashing as I heard them say, "Police! Pull over. . . . Pull your vehicle over now!"

Cathy complied. Then she did the unexpected. She lied . . . not about one thing but about everything. The officers separated us after getting all the wrong information and then instructed me to get my children and stay away from Cathy.

"We'll follow you to her house, and as soon as you can get your children somewhere safe, you need to go and be x-rayed," the police officer said to me.

"I will," I told the officer. "I'll call a friend who lives close by to come and pick us up."

He asked if we lived alone, and I told him we do, but I'd go to my mother's house.

Minutes after we arrived at Cathy's house, she changed clothes, slipped on her leather coat, grabbed her purse off the bed, freshened her makeup, and was just about to walk out the door when Donnie came in. Donnie had been a friend since we were kids, and my blindness had never interfered with our friendship. He was still like a big brother I could depend on.

Cathy's daughter Lynn turned to her and said, "Mama, we can go and pick up your friend so you won't have to go back out tonight. What if your assaulter is out there waiting to see if you're going to come out?"

"Don't be silly. I promised I would pick her up, and I'm going to do just that," Cathy responded.

"Ms. Cathy," Donnie said, "I'm looking at Jean, and her face is all bruised on the right side. Your skin is white, and I don't see one bruise on you. Can you tell me why? Why would someone beat a blind woman like this and never touch the sighted driver, not even once?" He told the girls to come with him, but he continued when he turned to face Cathy again at the door and asked, "Why didn't he take your purse too, and why do you feel so safe going out again tonight alone?"

Cathy didn't respond to the questions Donnie asked. She simply said, "I'll be back later," and went out the door.

Donnie turned to me and said, "Let's go." Donnie never raised his voice, but he was angry, and there was no doubt about it. If something were to happen to my girls, I would never have forgiven myself.

It was a short ride to Mama's house, where I left the girls with Bae. I didn't want them to sit in a hospital not knowing what was going on, and at Mama's they could watch TV or play games if they wanted to.

Also, my cousin Lovie lived next door to Mama, and I knew without any hesitation, if they needed her, Lovie would be there. Lovie was now a mom with two children of her own, but just as we had done as kids, we still shared good conversations. Ron and I had gone to her house one evening for a card party, and the living room was full of friends and family. They were all surprised to see the blind guy whip their behinds in cards, so they constantly asked each other, "Is he really blind"?

Lovie called me the next day and said, "Ron is such a cool dude. We all had a good time, and I'm glad to see you so happy."

On the way to the hospital, my head felt like it had a pulse of its own, and every thump made me angry at myself for not waiting for Mama to take me to the bank as usual. Cathy wasn't a longtime friend, but for the past two years, I had grown very fond of her and her daughters. How do you know that you can trust someone? I hoped I was wrong about Cathy. No, it was even deeper than that. . . . I prayed that I was wrong.

Mama parked her car in the emergency room parking lot, and Donnie pulled his car in the spot next to hers.

"Do you need a wheelchair?" Donnie asked. "I'll get one for you."

"No, I can walk."

"Baby, why did he beat you up so bad?" Mama asked. "Did you try to fight him?"

"No, Mama. I didn't get a chance to."

We walked into the emergency waiting room, and thank God it was not a busy night. I heard Mama say, "Can I give you the information you need for the doctor to see my daughter?"

The receptionist responded, "Yes. Have a seat right here, and we'll get her in one of the rooms for the doctor to examine her."

It took only a few minutes before the nurse assisted me to the x-ray room. There were no skull fractures, but there was a great deal of swelling and bruising. The doctor announced when he entered the room, "I'm going to prescribe some pain medication for her, and because of the concussion, she shouldn't be allowed to sleep for more than two hours at a time. Does she have someone to watch her closely for a couple of days?"

"Yes. She'll be at home with me. I'll take care of her," my mother quickly responded.

I felt safe in Mama's bed at her house, where nothing and no one could hurt me. Still, I woke from a nightmare about someone attacking me again, but this time I would scream, unlike before, and someone will help me. The loud scream broke the silence in the peaceful house and disturbed everyone in it. I felt so helpless once again.

Mama was there in an instant, sitting on the side of the bed, saying, "It's just a dream. Everything will be alright. Don't worry; it's only a dream."

"I'm so sorry, Mama. You didn't trust her from the beginning. I should have listened to you, and none of this would have happened."

Mama said, "It's alright. Go back to sleep now. Try not to think about anything. You're safe here at home with me."

My heartbeat was slowing down now, and the pain medication was once again taking control.

***

The phone was ringing. Mama answered, and I could hear her soft voice in the living room.

"Ron, he beat her up so bad. . . . No, she's here with me. . . . Yes, I know she'll be glad to hear from you. I'll take her the phone."

"Hi, Ron," I said as I tried to adjust the pillows under my head. "How did you know I was here?"

He said, "I've been calling you at home for hours, and when I didn't get an answer, I figured I should call your mother's. . . . "Jeannie," as he would call me. "What happened to you? Are you alright?"

"My head hurts really bad, but the doctor said I'll be alright in a few days. Ron, when can you come home?" I knew he had a few more days in Washington, but I wanted him there with me.

He said, "I'll be on the next flight out of here, baby. Can you tell me what happened?"

"All I know is Cathy lied to me and the police," I explained. "Ron, she lied. He wasn't a Hispanic; he was a black man. She said he was short; he had to be tall, or he couldn't have reached under the seat, and his face did not pass mine. She also said he wore a wool coat, but the jacket had to have had nylon or rayon in it for it to sound like it did. It wasn't wool, Ron; it sounded like an Eskimo jacket. I could hear every move he made. Why didn't she tell the officers the truth?"

Ron replied, "I don't know, but I'll find out when I get home tomorrow. Get some rest now, and I'll be home soon. I love you."

"I love you too." I thought to myself, *We worked so hard to raise money for our chapter affiliate. What can I do to make up for the loss?* I could stand to lose my own money but not money that we so desperately needed for our chapter. *I'll work extra hard and raise as much money as I can from now on, darn it! I was responsible for that money. None of this would have happened if I had gotten a ride with someone else.*

Ron came in on the morning flight, and once again I felt a sense of safety. I told him that if Cathy was responsible for what had happened, she would have to answer to God, and her punishment would be great. Now I knew to leave her alone. She made me think she was really my friend, but that was all just a lie. I thought I was a good judge of character; somehow, I had totally misjudged her. Oh, what a lesson I had been taught, one that time would never erase.

Chapter 7

Follow Your Heart

I had forgotten what it was like to go to the beach and feel as if I were wrapped in the calm and stillness of the heavens above right here on earth, and then listen to the waves as they splashed on the shores to greet me. Ron had called and asked if I would like to go to the beach with his brother, Moochie, and his girlfriend.

"That sounds like fun," I said. "The girls are with their dad this weekend anyway."

"I'll see you at about eight," he said.

When we got there, the four of us walked and talked for a while. Then Ron and I went our separate ways and found a small hill that we climbed and found ourselves quite comfortable on.

"Hey, remember the birthday party I gave you?" I spoke quietly as we reminisced.

"Yes, I do," Ron laughed.

We both sat there and thought back to that day. Holidays came all during the year, but there was nothing like celebrating a birthday. I wanted to do something very special for Ron, and it made me feel so good to know that I had turned what would have been just another birthday into one that he wouldn't forget any time soon.

We invited some of his friends and a couple of my relatives, which gave us a small, intimate group. We partied until very late, listening to music, playing cards, and sampling the variety of finger foods I had prepared for that night. The basement party was a surprise to Ron, and everything went as planned except for the few minutes when Ron had a lapse in memory. We had gone upstairs to the living room, where my cousin Jerry was. Both Ron and Jerry had had at least one drink too many, but they would have never admitted that. Ron, who usually didn't talk with his hands, tilted his cup in my direction, spilling his drink on me and the carpet.

"Ron, I think you've had enough for now. You're making a mess," I said.

He quickly responded, "I'll drink as much as I want to." And to prove it, he took another sip and added, "If you don't like it, you can leave!"

I thought to myself, *This man has lost his mind*, but I replied, "Did you forget this is my house?"

It took Ron a second to figure things out in his foggy mind, but then he said, "Oh yeah, that's right."

I said, "Now, if the two of you will go back downstairs to the party, I can clean up this little mess and join you all in a minute." I made some soapy water. I kept my left hand dry so I could find the wet spots and used my right hand to rub the carpet with a cloth.

After, when I got to the bottom of the stairs, I stood there until I knew where Ron was. I walked over to him and took his hand. "Would you like to dance with me?"

He never said a word but stood to his feet, took a few steps, and pulled me in close to him, which was right where I wanted to be.

"Thank you for the party. I don't know how you got all this together without me suspecting something, but I want you to know I had a good time," Ron said as he leaned down a little to give me a kiss.

Now thinking about it, his birthday celebration was a reflection of how close he and I had grown. He meant the world to the girls and I, and I wanted to make his birthday mean as much to him, as he did to us.

I grabbed his hands as we talked about everything that mattered to us at that moment. We talked about the two of us and what we wanted our lives to be like together.

"Do you think Lisa and Latrice would like to have a little brother or sister?"

"I think they would love it, and so would I."

"I'll always do what's best for you and the girls. You do know that, don't you?"

"Yes, I believe you will."

The moment was interrupted by Moochie yelling to us from a little distance away. "Are you two lovebirds ready to go?"

Ron called back that we were. He jumped down off the small hill first and instructed me to take his hands so he could help me down. I did as he instructed, and as soon as my feet touched the ground, Ron's arms were around my waist.

"Do you know how much I love you?"

"Do you know how much I love you?" I replied back to him.

The ocean, the stars, and this moment could not have been more perfect.

***

This is not good. Who in the world would be calling me at five minutes to twelve when All My Children *is coming on in five minutes? Whoever it is, they'd better keep it short.* I picked up the phone in my bedroom. "Hello?"

"Hey, baby," Ron's voice on the other end said. "I need to ask you a question." I had never heard him sound more serious.

"Ron, is everything alright?"

"Yes. I want to ask you if you will marry me."

"Are you serious?"

He answered, "Yes, I'm serious. Will you marry me? I'm at the phone booth at the courthouse on one knee. Will you please say yes so I can get up from here? People are asking me what I'm looking for. They think I've lost something. Please say yes! I'm going to stay down here on my knee until you say yes."

"Would you please get up?" I couldn't believe he was doing this at the courthouse.

"Not until you say yes," he said.

"Yes, Ron," I said "Yes! Now, please get up!"

"She said yes!" he announced. "I love you, Jeannie, and I'll see you when I get off work!"

"I love you too, Ron. See you this evening!"

I turned towards the television and realized that I had missed a good deal of *All My Children*, so I turned it off and fell back on my bed. I said, "Oh Lord, I'm going to be Jean Brown! I'm going to be Mrs. Ronald Brown!"

To some he may have been just an average guy, but to me he was everything I had prayed for. He had a romantic side to him that was very gentle, caring, and patient, which was just the opposite of what his friends knew of him. His buddies knew he had plenty of street sense and was definitely a ladies' man, but none of that mattered to me.

I'm going to be his wife. Oh gosh, someone is ringing the doorbell. I sat up on the bed, wondering who that could be. Standing up quickly, I rushed to the side door where I asked, "Who is it?"

The man on the other side of the door said, "I have a delivery for Ms. Jean."

The phone started ringing. I asked the man outside to wait a moment and grabbed the kitchen phone. "Hello," I said as I turned the key to unlock the deadbolt lock.

Ron was saying, "You have a delivery coming in a few minutes."

The man handed me a box and said, "I hope you enjoy your roses. Would you like me to read your card?"

"Yes, I would!"

He removed the card from the envelope and said, "There are flowers along the left side of the card, and the print says, 'To my one and only love,' and it's signed 'Ron Brown.'"

I took the card from the delivery man and said, "Hold on a second." I went back up the two steps and reached onto the kitchen counter where I had placed a five-dollar bill the day before. I opened the door and gave it to him. "Thank you," I said as I closed the screen door and locked it and the inside door.

I returned to the phone, trying to hold it on my right shoulder so I could have both hands free, and said, "Thank you!" I was opening the box, which had a big beautiful bow around it. "Long-stem roses!" I exclaimed.

Ron explained that they were pink and yellow. "I wanted to say thank you for saying you will marry me. I want to make every day of your life a happy one. I love you so much, and that will never change."

I took my time and arranged the dozen roses in the tall vase at the kitchen counter, and then took them to the dining table. What a lovely centerpiece they made.

I pushed the button on my alarm clock so it would announce the time. It would be only another hour and twenty minutes before Ron could leave work. He had told me he would be taking a cab to my house as it would be quicker than waiting on someone to be available to drive him. The tone of his voice indicated how frustrated he was, so I replied, "Don't worry; I'll still love you an hour from now. So I'll see you then."

An hour later, I heard a car door close in front of the house, and I knew it had to be Ron. I went to the door, and as soon as he rang the doorbell, I opened the door.

"There's my bride to be," Ron said.

"So this whole day has been for real? I'm really going to be your wife?"

"Yes, you are," he said. "To have and to hold until death do us part."

We put our arms around each other and exchanged a very long, passionate kiss that told us both we'd better get married real soon or we'd surely burn.

"I'm sorry I don't have a ring to give you yet, but I will soon," Ron said. "I'm going to adorn you with diamonds and pearls for many years to come."

"None of that matters right now. It will all happen in time. I made spaghetti and meatballs for dinner. Would you like a plate?"

"I sure would," Ron responded. "That smells so good. Girl, you know I love your cooking."

"Here's the garlic bread and a bowl of salad. Which dressing would you like?" I asked. "I'll have whatever you're having," he responded.

I took the silverware out of the drawer and got a couple of napkins for us. "Did you have a busy day?"

"No, it was actually a slow day, but hopefully next week will be better."

"Don't worry; it will. I don't know anyone who can resist the candy man," I said optimistically.

"Yeah, I know things will get better," he said, but I could detect the sound of concern in his voice.

I brought my plate to the table and asked, "So how soon can I tell Mama about our engagement?"

"Let's do that tomorrow. You, my love, can figure out which month you prefer and if this is going to be a small wedding or one that will break the bank."

"I promise not to go overboard, trust me. I'll cut costs wherever I can. Ron, we don't have to get married this year. We can wait until next spring or summer."

"Next year is fine with me," Ron said. "I've always wanted a summer wedding. What do you think about July?"

"That's fine as long as it's not on Latrice's birthday. You know she wouldn't be too happy if we take away from her special day." He agreed, and we decided the second Saturday of July would be our day to start our lives together as a family.

Ron was exhausted, and a few minutes after his right arm went around me to pull me closer to him, the sound of his breathing got softer. He was asleep just that quick, and I didn't have the heart to wake him. I sat quietly, lost in my thoughts about the relationship we shared. It didn't just appear to be a good one. It was filled with genuine love.

Chapter 8

All Is Fair

"Mama, it's Jean and Ron," I called as I knocked on her door.

"Here I come!" She yelled out, while opening the front door and talking to us before she could get the screen door unlocked.

"I didn't know you two were coming over here. Hi, baby!" She said as she gave me a quick hug, then reached out to Ron.

"How are you today, Ron?"

"Hi, Mrs. Williams. I'm doing fine, and you?" He replied.

"I'm doing fine. Thank you for asking," Mama said.

We both went to the living room and sat on the sofa.

"Mama, we would like to talk to you."

"Wait just a second. I need to put my roast back in the oven. I just finished putting the vegetables around it." She continued to chat while she was rewrapping the pan and informed us that my cousin Catherine was coming over. "She cooked a big pot of greens with smoked ham this morning, and she's going to bring me some."

"Sounds good! I hope she brings enough for you to share!"

Mama laughed. "You know she will. There's always enough left to put in the freezer."

I heard her close the oven door, so I knew she was on her way back to join us.

"Well, Mama," I said, "actually it's Ron who has something to talk to you about."

She had entered the living room and walked past us to get to her favorite chair.

"Alright, Ron," she said in her cheerful voice. "What would you like to talk to me about?"

He replied, "Well, Mrs. Williams, you know Jean and I have been seeing each other for a few years now, and I love her very much. I would like to marry your daughter and help her raise her daughters. I know we don't need anyone's permission, but we would both like to have your blessings."

"Mama, we want to get married in July of next year." I interjected out of excitement!

It was as if she didn't hear me. She got up from her chair and asked, "Do you two have thoughts about how difficult it will be for you as a couple? I mean, don't you think it would be better for both of you if you married someone with sight so they could help you?"

I thought to myself, *This is crazy. We don't need permission or blessings. We are two adults who love each other and want to build a life together.* I had married the father of my children one month after my eighteenth birthday, and as much as we had loved each other, our marriage fell apart. Neither my sight nor the lack of it could have made our marriage last. I prayed quietly to myself, *Please just be happy for us.*

I put my hand in Ron's and said, "Mama!"

But I didn't get a chance to finish my sentence. Ron interrupted, "Mrs. Williams, I wasn't looking for a blind girl to fall in love with. Yes, it may be hard sometimes being a totally blind couple, but I do know that marrying someone sighted wouldn't give either one of us a guarantee that it would last or that we would be happy. I don't want to marry Jean because of her blindness but despite her blindness."

As Mama sat down again in her chair, she said, "Ron, I do believe you love Jean and will do all you can to make her happy."

I looked across the room at Mama, and knowing how she could always read my expressions, I knew she could see how much I wanted her to be on our side. If no one else got it, I desperately needed our parents to. I didn't imagine us living a life without some struggles, but even the sighted couples we knew had problems, and they managed to work them out. Why would we be any different?

"So— there's going to be a wedding in July?" Mama said as if she was just confirming the month, but I could hear the excitement in her voice. "I want both of you to be very happy and take good care of each other!"

"Well, it looks like we have a wedding to plan!" I stood up to give Mama a hug and whispered softly in her ear, "I love you, Mama."

"Thank you, Mrs. Williams," Ron said as he joined in, and we had a quick group hug. "Have you told the girls yet?"

"No. I won't see them until tomorrow evening when they get home," I answered. "That's not the kind of news I want to share with them over the phone."

***

Lisa and Latrice's father had called to let me know he would be bringing them home in another few hours, to which I responded positively. My response was always understanding because I had the girls all week, and I knew how important it was for him to spend quality time with them also. I breathed a very short sigh and then thought, *It's only six o'clock. I could have all the cords cut for at least half the order before they get home.* I placed the scissors and yardstick on the kitchen counter and started measuring the cords.

The owner of a restaurant had ordered ten planters that were all to be identical—twenty-four inches long, made to hold a pot that would be fourteen inches in diameter. She explained, "I'm redecorating and would like to hang one over every other booth with a pot of greenery in each one." She had offered a little more information, not wanting to rush me or seem pushy. "My friend didn't tell me that you are blind." Then she added, "The painters will be finished in three weeks. Do you think you can have them made by then?"

"Mrs. Cross, my schedule is rather busy right now, but I'll have your order completed and ready for pickup in two weeks. I got the impression from her tone that she was thinking, *Poor blind girl; I don't want to put time restraints on her. After all, she can't see what she's doing!*

My, my, my, I thought to myself, *what a surprise I'll have for you!*

My babies came in the door later on as usual, with hugs, kisses, and the weekend replay. "Daddy bought us pizza, and we had popcorn just like at the movies! We had so much fun, Mama!"

"I'm glad you had a good time with your dad, but I sure did miss you two," I said with a big smile. "Come on, let's go to the living room. I need to talk to my two favorite girls."

"Mama, when did you get the pretty flowers?" Latrice asked.

Lisa stood at the table and asked, "Did Ron get those for you?"

"Yes, he did! That's part of the reason why I want to talk to both of you. Ron asked me to marry him," I said as I sat in the high-back gold chair at the living room entrance.

"When?" Lisa asked with excitement.

"Not until next year, baby." I answered their questions quietly. I no longer could just feel my heart beating; I could hear every thump.

Finally, the silence was broken, and the girls were grabbing my hands, pulling me up and shouting with all their lung power, "Yay! Mama's going to get married! Now Ron can stay with us! When can we see him so we can tell him we're happy, Mama?"

"Why don't we surprise him and go to his business tomorrow? I know he will be glad to see both of you," I replied. "Go ahead and put your pj's on and say your prayers. I'll be in there as soon as I put away these macramé cords."

They said, "We have to surprise him, Mama, so don't say anything when we go to his business tomorrow."

"I promise I won't," I told them as I locked pinkie fingers with each girl and shook on it, sealing the promise.

The next day, I was just as excited to visit Ron at work as the girls were. According to Lisa, the city bus wasn't crowded, and it didn't take very long to get downtown.

"Mama, I see him at the counter," Lisa said excitedly.

"Alright, girls, just remember—don't be loud because this is a business."

"We know, Mama."

Lisa opened the door. They went to the counter and asked, "May I have a bag of salt-and-sour potato chips with an orange soda please?" She was trying to use her big girl voice so Ron didn't recognize her, until Latrice added, "I want a bag of those chips too, but I want red soda and a bag of M&Ms."

Ron looked slightly confused. "Latrice . . . Lisa . . . what are you two doing down here? Where is your mom?"

Before the girls could respond, I asked, "what does a girl have to do to get some service around here?"

He smiled. "Just keep standing there looking beautiful, and you can have anything you want."

Chapter 9

Wedding Plans

"We have an appointment to meet with the pastor next week, Ron." There was no response from him, so I continued, "Will you be available on Thursday?"

He cleared his throat and asked, "What is this meeting for?"

"We do have a wedding to plan, you know?"

"Thursday will be fine. Jean, what if he doesn't want to marry us? I mean, what if he thinks I don't have enough to offer you and the girls? Then what? I can't even afford to get you a ring yet."

I said, "I wish you would stop worrying so much. How many times do I need to tell you, it will work out in time if it's meant to be. Ron, next year will roll around, and everything will fall into place."

I pushed the button to end the call, but I made no attempt to get up from the kitchen stool to hang it back on the wall. I just kept repeating to myself, *Lord, my faith is in you to work all things out. Please do it for us.*

***

"Are you nervous?" I asked Ron as we walked into the church.

"No. Should I be?"

"Of course not," I replied.

Someone came towards us with keys jingling and papers rattling. The sound of her heels clicked as she took several steps, stopped, and then again started in our direction. "Hello. The pastor will be out in a minute. He's just finishing up a call."

"Thank you," we both said simultaneously.

I turned my head to face Ron again. "Our next major project is to put together a guest list."

His response was simple. He stated that I could invite anyone I wanted to; it was fine with him. "No matter what you do, I'll show up," he said.

"That's so nice of you," I said in a tone that told him that was not the response I was looking for.

"Pastor will see you now," a voice said from across the room.

"Saved by the bell," Ron joked with a short chuckle.

As we entered the pastor's office, he took some papers and tapped them on his desk. "Well, hello, my child, and Ron, it is so good to meet you."

"Yes sir. It's good to meet you too," Ron said as they shook hands.

"Have a seat. There's two chairs just a little to the left of where you are now," Pastor said as he sat down and rolled his office chair closer to the desk. "So, Jean has told me that you two want to get married."

"Yes sir, we do!"

"Well, what do you do for a living, son?"

"I own my own business," Ron replied, "I'm a vendor at the courthouse downtown."

"Well, that's good you have a job so you can support yourself. A lot of people with a disability can't work. Have you thought about how hard it's going to be for you and Jean as a married couple? You need to take into consideration the lifestyle she is used to living. You can't even get her to the store or take her places she may want to go. Have you thought about that?"

The pastor's voice was calm, but there was a sense of concern that told me he didn't know anything about blindness and that he thought his questions were appropriate. I knew it was up to us to show everyone how capable we were, that we could manage on our own, but neither one of us was prepared for what we had just heard.

Ron moved a little closer to the edge of his seat and said as calmly as possible, "You know, Pastor, I work every day, and I can provide for Jean and her daughters. You see, I'm blind, not helpless. If Jean needs to get to the store or go out on the town, there are people who will drive us all day as long as we can pay for the service they provide. Now,

Pastor, you may know some people with a disability, but you don't know me. I've never experienced any missed meal cramps before, and I don't plan to in the future."

The phone rang. The pastor excused himself and took a moment to answer. When he hung up, he addressed us. "I know you two want to get married, and if you want me to perform the ceremony, I would be honored to do so. I just hope you both realize it won't be easy for you."

"We'll be fine, Pastor; we'll be fine," I said as I stood to shake his hand.

Ron stood and reached his right hand across the desk. "Thank you for agreeing to marry us, Pastor. Jean really wanted to get married in her church," Ron said.

"I think you've got yourself a good man," the pastor said as he shook Ron's hand and patted Ron's arm with his left hand. "I'll be happy to make the church available for your wedding ceremony. Just let me know the date and time."

I didn't know what made him have a change of heart, but that gave me a little assurance. We walked out of the church holding hands. The premarital counseling session was not at all what either of us expected. "Ron, if he doesn't want to marry us, we can ask your mother's pastor. He just doesn't understand," I said. "No, we didn't have all the answers, but we knew one thing for sure: we'd work it out because we loved each other that much."

"Jean, don't worry; we'll prove them all wrong," Ron said to me.

"I know we will."

***

There was never a dull day with Ron. He seemed to just enjoy having friends around, and a good cold beer was a must-have for those gatherings that would last until the wee hours of the morning.

I sat in the chair next to him at the card table and got lost in my own thoughts. I thought back to one night when he'd called me, and I told him that I was in the basement folding clothes. He knew I hated being downstairs at night alone, so he asked who was there with me. Obviously, I was alone, and I told him. I'd forgotten that earlier I had left a load in the dryer, but he didn't believe that. He tried to get a ride to my house, but no one would bring him, so he decided to set out walking. It was winter and the weather was dreadful, but anger and jealousy can make you do some crazy things. One of Ron's friends, Lorenzo, ended up dropping him off at my house, and to his surprise, I was the only adult there.

Ron came in and did a random search of the house, but all he found was my daughters. Lisa, who couldn't sleep, heard Ron pacing back and forth in the living room and instantly threw on a housecoat to go see what was going on. "I know someone was here," he kept saying while combing his hair and patting his Afro with the Afro pick he always carried.

After I confronted him, my response to his behavior and his accusations were, "Are you forgetting this is my house?" I looked at him and said, "Ron, I don't come to your house accusing you of anything, so you really need to think about what you are saying."

It had been a few years since that night, but Lisa never forgot. She would go through the living room, taking long strides back and forth, pretending she had an Afro and a pick, putting one closed hand that held the imaginary pick over the top of her head and the other patting her hair. She hadn't heard the conversation that night, but she certainly remembered what had happened and would laugh until she cried whenever she talked about it.

My attention was brought back to the present when Ron tapped my arm with his right hand and said in a whisper, "Watch me blow them away with this hand." And that was exactly what he did. I was happy for him, and I tried to ignore the low growls of his ever-present dog.

Etasha made sure I didn't make myself too comfortable whenever I came over to visit. Ron and I had a feeling that she had only one warm spot in her heart, and that was for him. If I sat in the living room, she would lie in front of the electric heater and watch me, and if

I was in the kitchen at the table, she would position herself right by the door so she could watch my every move. Ron told me that she could sense my fear, and that's why she growled and tried to intimidate me. *Well, look at her. She's a big red Doberman with red eyes, for God's sake. She can stop trying to intimidate me; she has already succeeded!*

Chapter 10

Working Together

"Alright, Madame President, let's get this meeting started!" Mamie and Laura, who were members of the National Federation of the blind and also two of my students at Tradewinds, were coming into the meeting room talking to everyone as they always did. Aunt Lee, Mama, and the girls were already seated, and the chairs around the long table were occupied for the most part. It seemed strange to not have Ron sitting to the right of me. Ron had served as NFB chapter president when Paul left, and I became the vice president. *I can never replace him,* I thought to myself. *Please hurry up and come back home. This is not where I should be.* I was very comfortable in the background doing the jobs no one else wanted to do. I had told Ron before he left that all I wanted to do was raise money for the organization. "You really shouldn't do this to me."

"You'll be just fine," Ron had said. "You know the philosophy as well as I do. You can handle it."

I told myself, *you'd better handle it, girl.* Ron had enough confidence in me to make me his vice president, and now that he was gone, I had to put on my big-girl panties and get the job done. I couldn't let him down, so I sat up nice and tall in my chair and called the meeting to order. It flowed just as smoothly as Ron said it would.

Ron had gone to Indianapolis to get some computer training, but it was pretty obvious to me that learning technology was not high on his list of interests. He would say, "I just can't move my fingers fast enough. It's like I always have to hunt and peck."

"You'll pick up speed soon. A few weeks will make a world of difference," I said. "Just hurry up and get finished so you can come home. The girls and I miss you."

"I miss you all too," he said, "but not for long. I'll be back home soon."

Paul had relocated to Indy and was loving his work there as a vendor in the Randolph Shepard Vending Program. Ron was staying with Paul while he was getting his training, and of course that meant going out to the bars, where they could get ice-cold beer by the pitcher. The two of them never had a boring day when they were hanging out together. Ron told me one day that Paul was the one who had taught him to travel around the college campus without using a cane.

"You see, what we would do is walk without losing a lot of contact with the ground, and then click your tongue against the roof of your mouth so you could bounce sound off the buildings. It's pretty cool. You can find openings too because the sound will keep going if there is nothing there to make it bounce."

"That sounds very interesting, but I don't think I would like to chance it," I said. "But if that works, why do you use a cane now?"

"Well, there comes a time in everyone's life when they have that 'come to Jesus' moment. As I was going down the hall in the Cooper Science Building one day, I had mine. I didn't know there were students on the floor on both sides of the hall studying. They had their legs stretched out, and because I didn't have a cane, even if they had looked up at me, they wouldn't have known that I was blind. Since the hallway was quiet, I was walking at a pretty good pace, until I heard this girl scream when I kicked her. I was walking into a lot of students, kicking books and people as they screamed and tried to move to safety. I got past all the students, and I heard someone running behind me. I thought, *I'm about to get my butt kicked for sure now*, but instead he slapped my back and said, 'Hey, man, that's some good stuff you're on!' I told him I wasn't high; I was blind. I had no reason for him or anyone else to believe me. I had painted a picture for the world to see, and now I wanted them to have another view of me. What a shame. Everyone knew I was blind except me. I wanted to pass. I still had the need to be accepted, and I wasn't sure I would be as a blind man."

I laughed until I cried, but in all the laughter, I understood Ron's pain, just as he understood mine. "Ron, is it really going to be as hard for us to make it as everyone thinks?"

"I can't answer that, Jean, but I believe if we love and trust each other enough, we'll be together until we're old and gray with false teeth in cups by our rocking chairs." We both laughed at the thought of that, and then Ron added, "We'll be together, Jean, until God calls us home."

"I love you so much. Will you try to come home next weekend?"

"Yes, I'll try, but you know it depends on how much work I have to do."

"I hate to go," I said, "but I've got a full day planned for tomorrow."

"Call me once you've made it back home."

"You know I will. Good night, Ron."

***

The months were starting to go by quickly, and although we hadn't made a lot of definite wedding plans, I hoped and prayed that everything would work out in our favor. Mama and I had spent the better part of a day shopping for a wedding dress, and that was as fun the second time around as it had been the first. Ron and I had discussed the colors and agreed that a solid white dress was out of the question. We decided on off-white for the primary color, and blue would be the accent color.

"You will be beautiful no matter what you wear," Mama said to me.

"Thank you, Mama. I think I'm just getting a little bit nervous."

"Let's get something to eat. We can talk about what you want to buy now or if it needs to be ordered. Then we can pick out the invitations and accessories for the wedding and the reception."

"I'm so glad you're here to do all this with me, Mama," I said as we walked out of the store, going through a list of restaurant names to choose from so we could get reenergized. Being in love and having a perfect wedding was getting more and more expensive. Ron still wasn't where he wanted to be financially, but he was determined to make it up that invisible ladder of success, and I would support him every step of the way. He'd be home soon, and things would be back to normal for us. Aunt Lee was still coming over to help with the house and was eager to get back in the kitchen to make more of Ron's favorite meals.

With a big smile on her face, she said, "I know you like your old aunt's cooking, Jean, but Ron really enjoys his meals." She was right, and both his family and mine knew that to be a fact. He worked hard, played hard, and ate heartily, so it was a pleasure to cook for him.

While Aunt Lee busied herself in the kitchen, I started working on Ron's wedding gift. I had decided to make a briefcase for him. Every businessman needs a good briefcase, and he didn't own one.

"I think he will love it, Jean. You do such good work," Aunt Lee said sweetly.

I was caught up in my thoughts now and said, "I'll have the leather store dye the pieces black and engrave his name in the leather. I can have the letters dyed in gold."

I had never made a briefcase before, but there was plenty of time to get it finished. It would be a good learning experience. Doing crafts had taught me a lesson that I needed to acknowledge, and that was the more difficult you think something is, the more difficult it becomes. So I looked at each piece carefully and pictured it as a completed product.

I put the briefcase aside and started working on another project that someone had commissioned me for. The table made with two twenty-two-inch rings and four rods that were eighteen inches high were covered with macramé cord. The cord's shape was taking on that of an hourglass in the center with diamond patterns, and the rods were covered with a spiral knot. It was truly a work of art, and the red and white design was elegant. The tabletop and the hanging table were the same size, with the diamond pattern and a Chinese crown at the top. It took days to complete each piece, but the look of satisfaction was written all over my face upon completion. And my generous pay made me believe even more that my craft wasn't just a hobby but a skill that had excellent benefits. I wanted each knot to be perfect and every customer satisfied. Mission accomplished!

Chapter 11

The Course of Life

I was running down a long corridor that appeared to be well lit. Someone was running with me. It seemed like such a long distance. I was trying to get somewhere, and finally I arrived. There was a set of double doors with oblong glass on either side of the long door handles, and the lady standing at the door was shaking her head no. I didn't know what she was saying, so I continued to pull the door handle. The door wouldn't open, so I moved along the right side of the wall, kneeled down, and cried, "Mama!" I woke up crying.

I told Mama about my troubling dream. "What do you think that dream was all about?" I asked.

"Well, baby, I don't know, but I can tell you this: God has a way of preparing us for all things, and if it made you cry, He will heal your heart."

"I'm just glad it was a dream and not for real, Mama."

I thought about how fast my heart was beating. No, it wasn't beating; it was pounding, and I don't ever remember crying that hard before. Mama was right, though. It was just a dream.

***

The new year had made its entrance, and the happiness and expectations for what it would bring were overwhelming to me at times. Lisa was wearing the title of teenager now. Had she completely outgrown her little tomboy stage? She was talking to me about some boy at school, but she didn't say anything about dating. She asked, "Mama, can we go skating this weekend?"

I replied without any hesitation, "Yes. As long as you get your homework, that's fine with me. I've got three wallets to get finished by Sunday of next week, so I'll have a needle in my hand all weekend."

Lisa replied, "I can help if you want me to." She was walking closer to the table as she continued saying, "Mama, Daddy said he would pick us up if it was alright with you, but he would have to bring us back tonight because he has to work all day tomorrow."

"Let him know I said it's fine with me, and if he wants to take you girls someplace next weekend, I don't have anything planned. Just tell him to give me a call later on in the week."

"Okay, I'll let him know after I finish shining this piece of leather for you."

The girls loved to roller-skate and having their dad out on the floor with them teaching them new moves made their faces light up with excitement. Skating and bowling were the two activities the three of them enjoyed doing together. It was his father–daughter time, and with his busy schedule, it pleased me to know he would always find a way to make time for his girls. No matter what our differences were with each other, the one thing we shared was our love for our daughters.

Ron called to let me know he had made it home. "Hey, baby, you want some company?"

"Yes, I would love to have some company!"

"Good. I'll be there shortly. My mother is going to bring me over."

"Alright, I'll see you then."

Before long, I heard the car doors close and I rushed from the bedroom to the side door. "Good morning," I said as soon as I unlocked the storm door.

"Well, good morning," Mrs. Brown said as she took a step forward to give me a hug. "Would you like to come in?" I asked.

She replied in her usual pleasant voice, "No, I can't this time. I've got some errands to run, but I'll see you two later." She turned, gave Ron a quick hug, and said, "Call me if you need a ride, Ron . . . and bye, Jean."

"Come on in, handsome. It's been so lonely here without you," I said to Ron.

He pulled me close to him. "I missed you more than you know. Are the plans for the wedding coming along fine?"

"Yes. Our invitations will be back in three weeks! Do you think your mother will help me get a list together of your family members?"

"Sure she will. Just give her a call. If there is anything you need her to do, Jean, just ask. You know she loves you."

"The store that's printing our invitations is giving us twenty-five extras at no cost. I thought that was so nice of them."

Ron asked, "So how many did we get?"

"Two hundred and twenty-five, and they are beautiful. I can't wait until they're delivered so you can see everything."

Ron replied, "Jean, what do you mean when you say 'everything'?"

"Well, the invitations, napkins, souvenir matchbooks with our names on them . . . and let me show you what Mama and I got already—"

"Jean, you said you would keep the costs down. What are you doing?"

"Please don't get angry—not today, Ron. Let me plan a beautiful wedding for us. I've had a wedding before, but you have never been married. I want both of our families to be there along with all our friends to celebrate with us. Trust me to take care of this," I said while reaching over to give him a really tight hug.

"I'm not angry," he said. "I love you too much to get angry with you. Now, let's see what you've bought already."

***

Mama hadn't been feeling very well for the past three or four days, and although she said she was hungry, she didn't eat very much at all. I called my sister Dora and asked if she could go over to Mama's house later. I went on to tell her, "Aunt Lee said she just doesn't seem to be getting any better."

That evening, I could hear the concern in my aunt's voice. At that moment I felt like that young girl whose life was in shambles as it had been so many times before when we didn't know if Mama was going to be alright or not. I tried to keep calm and had to admit it was hopeless.

God can do anything but fail. I knew in my heart that He could heal her. I just had to trust and believe in His power, so I kept repeating that to myself as I walked from the bedroom to the kitchen to get Mama a glass of ice water. Aunt Lee was sitting in Mama's recliner watching over her as she slept for five or ten minutes at a time. Her breathing was shallow, and she said it hurt so bad to breathe.

I heard a car stop in front of Mama's house and then the sound of car doors closing. "That's got to be Dora and the kids." I set the glass on the nightstand and left the room.

"Hi, Sister." That was Dora's usual greeting. She entered the house and gave me a hug.

"Dora, Mama's really sick, and I don't know what to do to make her feel better. The medicine for her cough is not helping her."

Dora turned to face her children and instructed them to go in the living room and be very quiet. "Remember, I told you all that Mama is not feeling well." Afterwards she made her way up to Mama's room.

Dora gave a hug to Aunt Lee and then stood at the side of Mama's bed in silence. In an attempt to keep the noise to a minimum, I had all the children leave the living room and go to Bae's bedroom. It was usually off limits unless she invited them in, but this time I knew she would make an exception. It was not always easy to keep the talking and laughter down, but somehow it was peaceful until Michelle cried out in a low, hoarse voice. They were young, but they understood something was very different about this visit to their grandma Pearline's house.

"I'm going to call her doctor. Maybe he can prescribe something else," I said to my aunt and sister. "Darn it! It's his answering machine. Dora, what do you think we should do now?"

"Let's wait for a while to see if he'll call back."

All the children stopped talking when they heard the doorknob of Bae's bedroom turn, and suddenly I was being bombarded with questions from every child in the room except the youngest, who was too little to understand what was going on.

Aunt Lee called me to Mama's bedroom. "She wants to talk to you, Jean. I'll be in the living room with Dora if you need me."

I sat on the side of the bed and asked, "Mama, can I get something for you?"

"No," she said softly. "Baby, do you remember where my insurance papers are, and my bankbook?"

"Yes, Mama. I'll take it all home with me until you come back home." I held her hand and told her, "You'll be alright, Mama. You'll be back before you know it."

She must have a fever, I thought to myself. *Her hands are so warm.*

She turned to me and asked, "Jean, will you call my children and tell them to come home?"

"Yes, Mama. Please try and rest so you won't keep having such a hard time breathing." Aunt Lee was back at the door again watching over Mama, taking care of her as much as possible as always. "Let me prop the pillows up a little more for you," she said.

"Dora," I said, "Mama wants us to call Bae and Arthur. She wants them to come home."

I dialed Arthur first and said, "Mama's very sick, and we are going to take her to the hospital, but she wants you to come home."

He replied, "Jean, is she that ill?" His tone was filled with disbelief.

"Arthur, please come."

He said, "I'll be on the next flight there. I love you all, Jean. Don't worry; Mama will be alright."

We said our goodbyes, and I placed the receiver on the phone. I knew that in Dora's silence, she was praying for Mama. I felt deep down inside that she needed every sincere prayer she could get.

My hands were shaking as I dialed the campus for Bae. "Hello, this is Arnetta Williams's sister Jean. I need to get a message to her that our mother is very ill, and we need her to come home as soon as possible."

Immediately, those words registered and sent a chill through my body. I felt the tears flowing down my face. Dora reached over to the stool where I sat and hugged me. Attempting to be strong, I tried to push Mama's words out of my mind when she had said to me, "Baby, always be there for your sisters and your brother."

"Mama, you'll be back home soon. You'll be alright."

"No, I'm not coming back here. I'm going home. I only wish I knew who will be here to help you."

"I'll be alright Mama," don't worry about me. I love you so much," I said as I gently touched her arm.

Mama was my best friend. I thought back to the last time I was with her, my sister Bae, and my brother Authur. We had planned a trip to visit my brother Authur in Virginia. I asked her if she wanted to fly or take the long bus ride. It didn't take long for Mama to respond, "No, I think the bus ride will be more fun. We can stop in all the other cities along the way and get something to eat and buy souvenirs. The kids will love it," she added.

"Alright, Mama, we'll ride the bus, but remember, this may not be fun after about ten hours on a crowded bus." I left the room before Mama could say anything else to try to convince me.

I tapped a couple of times on my sister's door to let her know I was about to enter the room. As soon as I swung the door open, I announced to Arnetta and the girls that we would be taking a trip to Virginia in July for a week. The cheers and high-pitched squeals filled the room as the girls held hands and jumped up and down, singing over and over again, "We're going to Virginia!"

"Well, the girls are all excited," I told Mama and then realized she was on the phone.

"The middle of the month will be perfect. We'll let you know what time our bus will arrive so you can pick us up from the station." There was a short pause, and then Mama continued, saying, "I will be fine on the bus. You know I like to take road trips. We'll call you back when everything is all planned!" The excitement in her voice about the trip was equal to that of the children in the other room, just not as deafening.

The weeks passed quickly, and we were ready for our visit. We took along some little hand games that could be played on the bus so the girls kept themselves occupied when they weren't sleeping. Arthur met us at the station as planned, and when we arrived at the house, my beautiful sister-in-law was there waiting for us. Mama and I had both had a good cry when we saw Arthur, and now here we were replaying the scene all over again. The children came running down the stairs, each one of them giving us hugs and kisses.

Talitha, the oldest, said, "Aunt Jean, Grandma Pearline, oh, I'm so glad to see you all!"

Mama said, "My goodness, the older you get, the more you look just like your mother. I'm so glad to see you again!" And before the conversation could continue, Tarana, Pearle, and Jr. entered the room, and more hugs and kisses were given to each of the children. A few minutes later, they all left the room and went up the stairs to entertain each other while Arthur prepared a smorgasbord of seafood and a variety of sides for us to enjoy.

Everything was perfect. Our trip was around Latrice's sixth birthday so we were all happy to celebrate my youngest girl. Arthur went out to get an ice cream cake for the celebration. Her uncle had just made her day!

"You should open a restaurant one day," I told my brother as he made a dressing for our salad.

"Maybe one day," he replied. As he began rolling the lemons, the scent filled the air, and I couldn't wait for a glass full of lemonade.

There was not one uneventful day in Virginia. We toured the city and got some shopping done, of course; caught up on what had been going on with each other; and still found time to indulge in my brother's good home cooking. The children had nothing more important to do than have fun, and that was exactly what they did for the entire week.

The time went by much too fast, and even though we talked on the phone often, it was not the same for any of us. "Mama," I said as we settled in our seats on the bus back home, "would you like to live in Virginia one day?"

"Oh, I don't know if I want to leave Aunt Lee, and you know she's not going anywhere," Mama replied.

"Maybe we can talk her into it," I said. Then I thought to myself, *when has anyone ever been able to talk Aunt Lee into doing anything she didn't want to do?*

Ron was working at the courthouse, and if I ever relocated, I would miss him, and the girls would surely miss their father and the rest of the family. Maybe when they are older I can consider making a move that far away, I thought.

I knew that Arnetta would be going off to college one day, and Mama would be home alone. I had asked her to move in with us, but she always said, "You are still young, and one day you will get remarried. I would just be in the way."

I replied, "Mama, how could you say that? We love having you here, and I want you to be in a safer neighborhood and closer to us."

She said, "Don't worry about me. I'm fine, baby. I can still take care of myself. You know, I'm not that old. What if I decide to get a guy friend?"

I gave her a quick glance of disbelief that she didn't notice and replied, "Yes, I know, Mama." And that's how the conversation would always end.

"The ambulance is here, girls." Aunt Lee yelled from the kitchen, and it snapped me back into reality.

Dora gathered up all of Mama's medications and put them in a bag. I got her purse, took out the leather key ring I had made her, and locked the door behind me. I prayed, "She's got to come back home, Lord. Please, please let her get well."

Mama was admitted into the hospital, where they immediately began to draw blood, which was followed by x-rays and a series of questions to help them figure out exactly what the problem was.

Arnetta came back home as quickly as she could to be with Mama. She leaned over the bed rails and gave Mama a kiss on her forehead. "I'm here, Mama. Please get well," she said as she rubbed her hand on Mama's arm.

A nurse came in the room and announced softly, "I'll let you all stay here with your mother as long as you promise to let her get some rest." She paused as if she were waiting for a response, then said, 'I'll be back shortly."

The three of us quickly thanked her and moved to seats across the room. The nurse didn't have to worry. We wouldn't be talking to each other. We would be praying to God.

They gave Mama medication that helped with the pain but made her very incoherent most of the time. She woke up for a few seconds to talk to us and fell back to sleep before she could finish her sentence.

"Hey, sisters," Arthur said as he entered the room, making sure his steps were quiet so he wouldn't disturb Mama. He stopped at the side of her bed. "Do the doctors know what's wrong yet?"

"No. They haven't got the test results back yet."

Mama's voice was weak, but she managed to get a few words out when her son entered the room. "There's my son."

"Hi, Mama. I got something for you," he said as he held a white dog puppet over her bed. With his hand in the puppet, he said, "I've got a surprise for you, but you have to get well to enjoy this one." He took the puppet off his left hand and said, "Mama, here's five hundred dollars for you to go on a shopping spree." He paused and then said, "You've got to get well, Mama. I don't know what we would do without you."

Mama put both hands down to her sides, and an odor filled the room as some of her organs shut down. We all started shouting for the nurse, and Arthur pulled the cord for someone at the desk to come help Mama.

"You all have to leave the room now! Please go to the waiting room, and I'll call you when you can see her!"

There were several days of visiting Mama in the intensive care unit. She had mittens on her hands and restraints on both of her wrists and ankles. I stood by her bed holding her hand while she slept, talking to her constantly so she would know I was there. I promised her that I would never leave her alone, thinking back to when she had been diagnosed with bone cancer, when I told her, "You will never have to go through anything alone, Mama. I'll be right there." I quoted some Bible scriptures to her just in case she had forgotten them or wanted to say them with me to be in agreement with someone. I didn't know what she could remember because she couldn't talk anymore.

"I'm sorry" the doctor said. "Your mother has pneumonia, and we don't know how to treat this particular kind. Her heart is weak, and I think she's getting tired of fighting."

"Please, don't give up on her," I said. "There must be something else you can do."

He walked towards me and touched me on the shoulder, and in the softest voice I'd ever heard him use, he said, "I will do everything I can to save your mother. Don't worry; I won't give up."

The four of us knew we would be lost without Mama, but at least we had extended family to comfort us. Arnetta had only us. How would she get through this difficult time?

Aunt Lee, Uncle Willie, and my cousin Katherine came to the hospital together, and we had a praying good time in the waiting room. It got so good, the family in the room next to ours came in and asked if they could pray with us. We didn't care about their race, their financial status, or their religious beliefs as long as they believed in God. We stood side by side and held hands as we prayed for our loved ones.

Chapter 12

Inseparable

Dora had been the driver for me and Aunt Lee each day to the hospital and then back home, and it was pretty clear that she was tired, although she never complained. We were never gone for long, and someone was always there with Mama. I checked my voice messages as soon as I got home just in case the hospital had called while we were gone. My friend Mary had left a message on my phone that said, "Call me back. I haven't talked to you for days now. Are you and the girls alright? Okay, it's Mary. I'll talk to you later."

The next call was from my friend Dee, saying, "I hope everything is alright with you." She sighed and said, "Well, maybe you are just too busy planning your wedding and you're just getting in too late to call me, but you better call me back, girl. I'm getting worried."

Ron and I had talked earlier, but there was a message from him as well saying, "Baby, call me when you can. I hope Mrs. Williams is doing better. Alright, call me."

I turned on my bathwater and went to my closet to get something out to wear. "Dora, do you need anything?" I asked. There was no response, and I realized my sister was sitting in the first chair she had gotten to and was sound asleep. I grabbed the throw from the foot of my bed and put it over her. She continued to sleep, and I knew that the hour of rest would do her lots of good. I wasn't going to wake her just to tell her to go to bed.

It felt so good to sit in the tub even though I didn't get to relax for long. It seemed as if everything had to be done in a hurry. *Oh well*, I thought, *this may be a good time to return my calls quickly before I leave out again*. I checked the time and realized we had been gone from the hospital for an hour already.

I'll call them back later, I thought. Our time was up.

"Hey, Sis, wake up. It's time to go."

"Where are Lisa and Latrice?" Dora replied.

"They're at their aunt's house. I don't want them to have to be at the hospital all day. They have both of their cousins to keep them company, and whenever I come home, they can run down here to see me." I stopped talking for a few seconds to take a deep breath to compose myself. I continued, saying, "I'll just be glad when Mama comes home."

"You know, the girls can come over to the house whenever they want to."

"Thanks, Dora, but you're doing enough driving already. Don't forget, you are on the other side of town now. Plus, girl as long as they are with family or friends, I know they are in good hands."

Arthur was standing at the entrance to the waiting room when Dora and I got back to the hospital. We asked, "Have you all heard anything from the doctor yet?"

"No," he replied as he put his arms around Dora and me. "I hate hospitals," he said as he walked out of the room and started down the hall. Walking at a very slow pace, he mumbled, "I'll be right back. I just need some air."

One of my dearest friends had come to the hospital to see if there was anything he could do or get for the family. Eugene Walker, who had known me since I was thirteen years old, walked into the room and started hugging the family.

He placed an arm around me, giving me a hug, and said, "God's love is your strength. Just don't let go."

"I won't. I can't, Eugene." I wiped away the tear that was making its way down my cheek and asked him, "Will you walk with me to the chapel?"

"Of course I will," Eugene said as he stood up. He asked, "Does anyone need me to bring something back?"

Everyone said no, and we began our long walk to the chapel.

"Here we are," Eugene said. The door was open, so I took my cane, walked down the center aisle, and kneeled at the altar to pray. I wanted God's undivided attention. I wanted to pour my heart out to Him. I had to make it clear how much my mother meant to not only me but to the rest of her children and family members. Why would He take her from us?

I began praying and said, "Lord, thank you for all your blessings. You have protected us from all harm and danger, seen and unseen. Lord, I thank you for your love, your Mercy, and your grace. Father, I come before you asking that you heal my mother. Lord, you said in your word that by your stripes we are healed. Please, Lord, do it for her. Let her get well and come home again. I'll do anything you ask, Lord. Please, just don't let her die. In the name of your Son, Jesus Christ, I pray. Amen."

I picked up my cane and started to leave where I had poured out all my feelings to the Lord, only to get two steps from the chapel and realize what I had done. It was as if my shoes had become a cement block and I no longer had the ability to move. "Eugene, I need to go back," I said with so much urgency in my voice, he didn't ask why. We immediately turned around. I had to ask Eugene to walk me back to make right a prayer that had been filled with all the wrong emotions: hurt, fear, loneliness, disappointment, and anger, none of which I had intended to offer up to God in prayer.

"Father, please forgive me, for I have prayed a selfish prayer. Lord, I thank you for blessing us with a wonderful mother who you loaned us for a time. Thank you for taking away her pain and giving her love, peace, and joy that she has never known. Father, I pray that your will be done in our lives, and that when my mother has taken her last breath, you will receive her unto yourself, for it is you who loved her first. In the name of Jesus Christ, our Lord and Savior. Amen."

I picked up my cane again and walked out of the chapel. I'm almost certain that I did not get any further down the hall this time than I had the first time. The halls were quiet except for the lady on the intercom saying, *"Code blue! Code blue!"*

"That's my mama!" I told Eugene.

"No, listen. It could be any of the patients in there. Please, you've got to listen to me."

"No, that's my mama," I said as my fast steps changed to running with Eugene arm in arm down the hall.

I watched my dream that had had me in tears a few months ago unfold. Mama was gone, and the pain was unbelievable. The pain I felt seemed to be pulling all the strength from my body, and my legs felt as if I couldn't stand. I told myself to pull it together. I knew if I was hurting this bad, my siblings had to be hurting too. *I've got to try and be there for them.* Then I thought to myself, *No, somehow we have to find the strength to be there for each other.* I wiped my eyes even though the tears continued to fall… and said softly, so only God could hear, "Thank you Lord, for loaning us our mama."

Each one of us made it through the days before the funeral by simply loving each other. We were just doing what we thought Mama would have expected of her children. There was no complicated estate to handle, so everything was divided between the four of us, and of course Aunt Lee was told if there was anything she wanted, all she needed to do was let us know.

We spent many hours going through Mama's belongings, but when we finished, each one of us walked out of her house with precious memories that would last us a lifetime and beyond. The relationship we had experienced with our mother had been one of love, admiration, respect, and friendship. It was all she had to offer of value, but it was genuine. Unlike most possessions, her love could never be devalued or replaced in our hearts.

Chapter 13

Season of Change

Delores was checking in on me every day, making sure I held onto my sanity and that the grieving period didn't take me under. I had learned to deal with total darkness, but the thought of Mama being gone from our lives was something I could not conceive. Even though it had been inevitable, there was no way to prepare for the emptiness her death had left behind. Delores, determined to lift my spirits every day, offered some words of scripture, a prayer, and kindness that seemed to hug me right through the phone.

Arnetta returned to school, trying with all her might to reassure us that she would be fine. It was her freshmen year in college, and she wanted to be independent. I got all of that, but I still cried when she left.

Arthur returned home and called to let me know he had made it safely. "I'm only a phone call away," he said.

"I know," I replied. "Tell the family I said hello. Hugs and kisses to you all, and I'll talk to you later this week."

I placed the receiver on the wall base and went to the basement with my daughters. It was then that God made me realize why I had to be strong. The girls were young, and they didn't quite know how to express their pain, but it was as real for them as the loving relationship they had shared with Mama. I stopped for a minute just to slow my thoughts down before saying, "Hey, girls, Ron should be on his way over. If you two pick out a movie, I'll gather up some snacks and bring them down for us."

"Okay, Mama. We'll find a good one for you!"

Ron was there shortly after I went to the basement with the snacks and put them on the coffee table in front of the sofa. I ran back up the stairs and opened the door.

"Hi, baby," he said as he wrapped his arms around me.

I thought to myself, *This is another reason for me to keep myself together. I love the three of them as much as they love me, and I certainly wouldn't want to live my life without them in it.*

***

Our wedding day was quickly approaching, and I wanted everything to be perfect. Our uncle on Mama's side of the family was going to stand in my brother's place, and although Mama couldn't be replaced, there was no one else closer to me than Aunt Lee, who would do anything to see me get to that peaceful place in life again. Without a doubt, Aunt Lee wanted Ron to be a part of our family and told Uncle Willie, "You know, they make each other happy, and that's all that matters." I knew then that she was trying to get the focus off our blindness and see us as any other couple in love.

When I asked my uncle if he would have the honor of giving me away, I was thrilled when he accepted. "Thank you. This means so much to me," I said.

The list of things to do was almost finalized. The invitations had been mailed out, the reception hall had been rented, the cake had been ordered, and everything for the bridal party and the bride-to-be had been taken care of.

"Ron, the only thing left to do is get your tux fitted and get the menu planned. I'm so excited everything is going so smoothly. We're going to have a beautiful wedding!"

"Yes, we are. It's your day, baby, and you can have whatever you want," Ron said in a happy, very sincere tone that made me smile.

There was always something to do to keep me busy, and boy, was I ever glad for that. There were about three weeks left before the big day, and Dora and Arnetta made sure there wasn't anything else to do except make sure the groom showed up.

"He will," I replied. But no sooner had I spoken the words when I thought, *He's never been married before. What if he gets cold feet?*

My expression must have said what I didn't dare say because the two of them looked at me and laughed. "We were just kidding."

***

I felt as if every nerve in my body were on edge, and I wondered how Ron was handling this day. I had talked to him before the bachelor party, and he sounded as excited about today as I was.

Aunt Lee knocked, opened the door, and said, "If you all are ready, we need to leave this room. Jean, you can wait in the balcony until it's time for the ceremony. Come on, I'll go up there with you. You girls look so pretty." She then added, "Your old aunt is so proud of you all."

The three of us stretched out our arms for a group hug and told Aunt Lee how much we loved her too. We made it up to the balcony and sat where we could not be seen by the guests who might arrive early.

When Ron's mother was styling my hair earlier that day, she told me how when her son had brought me over to meet the family, she had made up her mind that she was going to tell me off. She was not going to let another girl come along and hurt her son. She said, however, once she met me, she realized how wrong she was and decided to just let us figure out where our relationship would go. The curlers were clicking fast like Mama always made them do.

"I know I can't replace your mom, but I want you to know I'll always be there for you, and I'll always treat you like you're one of my daughters."

My eyes began to fill with tears as I quietly said thank you. I knew in my heart that God had put this family in my life for a reason, and I would love them always.

Aunt Lee placed her hand on mine and said, "I believe your mama is smiling right now. Her spirit is in this place, and she's filled with joy." I gave her a tight hug, and she said, "This is a happy day. You'll mess up your makeup if you start to cry."

I told her, "I won't, Aunt Lee. I promise."

It was absolutely amazing how Dora and my cousin Terry voices came together and captured the hearts of our guests when they delivered two songs that were absolutely beautiful. My uncle took my arm.

Arnetta placed a bouquet of flowers in my left arm and said, "Now you're ready." Arnetta said in a soft voice, "Jean, they're unrolling the runner for you now. Are you ready to go meet your groom?"

"Yes, I am. Thank you, Sis."

I would have been a nervous wreck walking down the aisle, but my Ron was up there, and I couldn't get to him fast enough. My uncle moved from my side when we reached the altar, Ron stepped over to take my hand, and all was well! My pastor was against the wedding in the beginning, but he could not have performed a more beautiful ceremony, and if I had to do it all over again, I wouldn't change a thing.

Our reception was immediately following the dinner at the church at a hall that would comfortably hold all the guests and leave plenty of room for dancing. We arrived at the hall and heard a voice coming from the kitchen. "Hi, sweetie. I'm going to have to give you a refund because there's no way you can have your reception here. Our air conditioner went out this morning, and we've got to finish cooking for an event tonight. As you can feel, it's got to be about a hundred and thirty degrees in here. We've got the doors propped open and fans everywhere just to circulate some warm air. I'm so sorry!" She had not slowed down for one second to give me a genuine apology. Her focus was on the dinner she was preparing, and I got the impression that nothing else mattered at the moment.

The dinner at the church had been superb and enjoyed by the older guests, who had given us their congratulations and were gone home. Our friends, on the other hand, had no thoughts of leaving. They were ready to party till the break of dawn, so changing the location would not matter to them at all.

Arnetta wrote a note that simply said, "The reception for Ron and Jean will be at her house. See you there!" She taped it on the door and said, "Don't worry. You and Ron are still going to have a reception."

All of Arnetta's creative juices were flowing as she hung the large wedding bell from the chandelier and put the blue and white tablecloth on the table. Dora put the sheet cake on the table while Ron and Mike, a good friend of ours, moved the coffee table so the champagne fountain could be in the center of the living room. The DJ set up the music in the basement, making several trips to his car and bringing in crates of records. The party was about to start, and everyone filled their glasses to toast the bride and groom.

Ron gave my hand a little squeeze and said, "Here's to the rest of our lives together, Jeanie." And we sealed that toast with a kiss.

We partied for hours and finally made our getaway with Mike promising to make sure all the windows and doors were locked before he left. No one could party harder than our blue-eyed soul brother. He would stay right there until the last record was played and the last person was gone. We could depend on Mike to take good care of things for us.

It was well after midnight when we left the reception for the honeymoon. The hotel suite was elegant, the wine was excellent, and the night was filled with all the pleasures I had anticipated.

Ron held me close and said, "You're a bad girl, Jeanie Brown. . . ."

And in my defense, I replied, "Yeah, but when I'm bad, I'm oh so good."

He said, "Oh yeah, you got that right."

It was late at night (or maybe early morning) when neither one of us could keep our eyes open any longer. *This is my dream come true*, I thought as I drifted off to sleep.

The sound of Ron putting the receiver back on the phone on the table next to our bed woke me up. As I reached for him, I asked, "You're up already. Is everything alright?"

He turned his body towards mine and moved the hair off my face. While giving me kisses he explained, "I'm up because I had to order us some breakfast. I have to take good care of my beautiful bride."

I hugged him and replied, "I know you will, and I'll take good care of you too. So what did you order me for breakfast?"

"Oh, just an omelet, toast, orange juice, and coffee. Does that sound good, Mrs. Brown?"

"That sounds excellent, Mr. Brown, especially since I didn't get to eat my dinner at the church."

"You didn't?" he replied.

"No. Someone tossed it when we went to cut the cake, so I'm really hungry now," I explained as I slipped on the plush robe provided by the hotel.

"I know you are," he said as he reached across the bed and grabbed the belt to the robe, pulling me right back down on the bed. We both laughed, and just as a pillow fight was about to begin, the waiter was knocking on our door. "You are so lucky," Ron said as he got up to answer the door.

We sat across the table from each other while we ate our breakfast. Ron broke the comfortable silence. "I'll always try to keep you happy."

I picked up my glass of orange juice. "I'll drink to that." We clicked our glasses together and took a sip. I smiled at him and told him, "I will always give you all my love." We clicked our glasses again and felt the presence of love all around us. I thought to myself, *God, you have been so good to us!*

***

"Aunt Lee, move to Indianapolis with us, please. I'm going to miss you so much," I told her as I put away the shoes and bags I had worn for the wedding and the reception.

"Baby, I like having my own place. I'll be just fine, and you can always come and visit me."

"Alright, but if you change your mind, I can help you find a place close by," I said with a look of concern on my face.

She replied, "If I ever need you to come home, you know I'll call you. I just want you, the girls, and Ron to get settled in and be really happy. There's no need for you to look so worried."

Aunt Lee got up from the dining room table and picked up her coffee cup. "I'm going to have a little more coffee, and then I'll get started cleaning the chandelier." Before I could say anything, she said, "It won't take long to do that, and if you want, I can help you get the girls' winter clothes packed up so they'll be out of the way."

"Yes, ma'am. That would help a lot." I took another sip from the coffee cup. "You've been a part of my life since I was four years old. I just lost Mama, and now I'm leaving you. Somehow it doesn't seem right."

"I'll be right here," Aunt Lee said, and I could imagine her big smile as she went on to say, "for as long as the Lord says so."

The four of us would be leaving all our family, our friends, and our church home to build what I hoped would be a lifetime of new ambitions and dreams that would make us all believe the move was meant to be. Ron and I discussed the desire to continue to support the Northwest chapter of the NFB despite the move. There just wasn't enough support being given to this part of the state by the training center or vocational rehabilitation services. If you didn't know the laws that pertained to blind people, didn't know how to advocate for yourself, and accepted whatever you were given without question, the truth was you wouldn't get a lot from the system that was supposed to be on your side. The Gary courthouse had been a learning experience for Ron and had given him the motivation he needed to be successful in business. I never would have relocated, but for Ron, this was just another adventure he felt compelled to explore.

Ron said, "You and the girls are going to love it there. There's so much to do and so many places for the girls to go. I checked around, and the school system is outstanding with lots of after-school activities they can get involved in. You can get them registered on Monday, and they will be all set for school when it starts."

He finally stopped talking to take a breath, so I asked him, "What day will we be moving?"

Without any hesitation, he answered, "I talked to the lady in the office at one of the apartment complexes on the south side, and she said we could move in next week! I know you haven't seen it yet, but Jean, trust me. I would never move to a bad area. I want you all to always feel safe."

"Yes, I know you do. And yes, we can be all packed up and ready to go by then!"

Time was winding down swiftly. Every call made to say goodbye—reminded me of someone else I hadn't called, and the packing seemed to never end.

"Dora, I'm going to miss you so much. Will you come down to visit us soon?"

"Now, Jean, you know we'll be in touch all the time," she said.

I took another stack of towels from the shelf in the linen closet to finish filling the box. "Well, Sis, I'll just have to make sure I've got the best long-distance phone plan available so we can talk whenever we want. You know I've got to follow my man."

We laughed and continued to talk for a while as we did almost every day. I needed to be optimistic about the future and hold onto the good memories, but as Grandma always told me, "As pretty as a rose is, remember there are also thorns to be aware of." I held onto the good memories, and I thought how incomplete our lives would be without them. Grandma died when I was seventeen, but her words of wisdom lived on forever.

It seemed as if every time I mentioned that Ron and I were relocating, someone would be surprised, and eventually I'd be asked, "How are you planning on making it in a strange city?"

I had a patient reply that put an end to their questions: "Oh, don't worry. We're just blind. We'll figure it out."

Once people saw by my response that we weren't worried, it seemed to help ease their fears. One thing was for sure: we weren't as intimidated about moving to a new city as they probably imagined. We were more than ready to move forward with the next chapter of our lives and to conquer our dreams and goals together.

Chapter 14

Adjustments

Ron got out of the car and went up the stairs to unlock the door. As soon as it swung open, the girls ran right past him to the bedrooms, asking, "Mama, can we have this room?"

I reminded them that I hadn't even looked at the bedrooms yet. I responded with, "Girls, please slow down and help Ron get some of the small items off the truck."

But they were excited and focused on other things like the patio. They pleaded, "There's a patio, Mama. Can we put some chairs out there?"

"Yes, we can, but it won't be today. Girls, I need you to stay focused. We are trying to get unpacked."

"Okay, Mama!" they both replied.

"Ron," Lisa asked, "where do you want me to put this bag?" Then she asked for something cold, while Latrice had grabbed the family-size bag of chips and decided to sit on the floor and take a chip break.

"I've got potato chips. Anybody want some?"

Ron decided we all needed to take a break. "Listen, we've been at it all day. Let's walk over to McDonald's. We can bring the food back here and watch a movie. Jean, don't worry; the boxes will still be there tomorrow."

"I know they will, but some things just have to be moved today," I said as I went to the room to get my cane. "Alright, let's go," I said as I came down the hall, using my cane to get around the boxes that were still on the floor. I was being extra careful because I knew my china was in one of them. Ron didn't know it, but I was planning to give our grandchild that set, especially if she liked to cook or have dinner parties. *I'll share that with him one day, but it won't be discussed anytime soon.* The apartment was cable ready, and we were all worn out and ready for some relaxation.

Ron started working at his new vending location, which meant an early start in the mornings cleaning and filling coffee machines. If you want an angry customer, let them get some bad coffee or, worse than that, let them get no coffee at all. Most of the customers were nice, though, and I enjoyed talking to them when I got the time to chat. I liked to find out what products they wanted in the vending machines

Ron asked, "Did I tell you what happened at work the other day?"

"No, you didn't," I said.

"There were two men in the hall talking, and when they saw me coming towards them, they stopped talking. I mean, it was almost like they held their breath or were hypnotized by the tapping motion of my cane. So when I got up close to them, I said in a really loud voice, '*Boo!*' I laughed so hard, Jean, they almost jumped out of their shoes. I think they thought that if they didn't make any more noise, I wouldn't know they were there. But that's alright; I'll educate them about blindness a little bit each day."

"You are so silly," I said, "but you're right, and they couldn't have a better teacher."

Ron's workday was finished early in the afternoon, so the three of us would sit at the table and count all the coins that came from the vending machines and that had to be rolled for deposit. Then, as usual, Ron would pull out a bag of goodies for us to enjoy from the business while we watched television. Of course, it didn't matter if there wasn't anything good on because that gave the girls another opportunity to watch one of their favorite movies: *Roots*, *Annie*, *The Color Purple*, or *The Godfather*. They would hit the rewind button over and over again so they could recite their favorite lines. They had Oprah's and Whoopi's parts in *The Color Purple* memorized word for word.

As a teenager, I had participated in a citywide program for kids where I studied drama at Indiana University-Purdue University

Indianapolis (IUPUI) Northwest. I had the privilege of making our costumes for the summer play. It gave me a real love for coordinating and planning the setup of the stage. Every little intricate detail mattered. It was more than what we wore; it was the hair, the makeup, and the lights, and it came right down to every single word one said.

Years later the excitement of being involved in theater prompted me to call Mama and tell her about a new playhouse in town. I told her, "I'd like to go and have the girls, Bae, and myself audition. I don't know if they will allow me the chance to get involved or not, but at least the girls can have some fun! Mama, I really want them to experience this, and I want to see how she will react to having a blind person in the cast."

Mama replied, "Alright, Jean. I'll be there at six to pick up my stars."

The four of us auditioned and were welcomed into the Morning Bishop Theater Playhouse. We dedicated many hours at home to learning our lines. Even though it wasn't for a Broadway stage, we took it very seriously. Mrs. Bishop, a teacher, writer, devoted mother, and friend who shared her knowledge and creativity in some way with everyone she met, gave us all a glow when the lights came on. She had a way of making everyone feel like a star while she was constantly working to perfect every production. Although the opportunity to act might never come along, I think she gave us all the confidence needed to be on stage if we wanted to.

Ron played with a "beep baseball" team and was as committed to the sport as any professional ball player. He had told me the rules of the game one day when he came home with a banged-up body that made him moan and groan each time he tried to move. "Did you win?" I asked.

"No, not this time, but there's always next year," he said.

Yes indeed, let's keep hope alive, I said to myself while I continued to rub one sore spot after another on his aching body. It's amazing what the love of the game will make a guy do if he is competitive enough.

The game had started for him the year after we met, and win or lose, each World Series defeat simply meant the team had to try harder and one day they would succeed. Yes, one day they would be champions.

Ron reassured me by saying, "Jean, the injuries are not that bad, and they don't happen that often. Man, to be out there running and tackling the bases, there's nothing like it. I love this game. When you can swing the bat and hit a ball just from listening to the sound of the beep inside it and then run to a base that beeps and score, it sends you on a natural high that you want over and over again. After losing my sight, I thought I would never play sports again, and then I was introduced to the game of baseball for the blind, a game where even if you have a little sight, it doesn't matter because everyone has to wear a blindfold so we are all on an equal playing field."

I could hear the passion in his voice and hoped that no matter how crazy I thought he was, he would keep his enthusiasm for the sport and his determination to win! He had earned the nickname Shotgun out on the field because he would hit the ball so far, the defense on the other team couldn't track it fast enough to stop him from scoring. I thought as I applied pain cream, disinfectants, and alcohol on various wounds that if he had not lost his sight, there is a possibility I wouldn't have met him. Would he have been a baseball superstar? I wondered if our paths would have ever crossed. I put the lids back on my medical supplies and began to massage his back. He moaned a little as a sign of relief and continued to sleep. *Well, Nurse Jean, looks like you've done all you can do at this time. The patient is resting quietly once again.*

A couple of days after we moved into our apartment, there was a knock at the door, and I could hear a lady's voice saying, "It's your neighbor from upstairs."

"Oh, just a minute!" I yelled out from the hallway. I unlocked the door and swung it open.

We extended our hands to greet each other as she introduced herself. "My name is Sharon. I live right upstairs on the next floor."

"I'm pleased to meet you. My name is Jean."

"Are those your two girls?" she asked. "They are so cute. I have two girls also," she explained.

One of her girls was calling her. "Mom, where are my black shoes?"

Sharon called back, "Girl, go look in your room!" She turned to me and continued talking, appearing to be a little flustered at her daughter. "I'm in a rush right now, trying hard not to be late for choir rehearsal, but I'll come down and introduce them to you and your girls this week if you'd like."

"That would be nice. I'm sure they would like that."

"I just wanted to tell you, if I can help you with anything, let me know," she went on to say.

"I will, and thank you for offering. That's so kind of you."

"Not a problem. See you later!"

I could hear the sound of her heels on the steps as I closed my door and went back to organizing Ron's closet. I thought to myself, *I hope the rest of our neighbors will be as nice as she is. Oh well, we will soon find out.*

"Hello?" Dora answered her phone in a very sharp tone. Her greeting was filled with anger or maybe disappointment. I didn't know which, but I knew something was wrong.

"Hi, Dora, are you alright?" I asked as I ran my fingers across the edge of the desk that was attached to a bookcase, which made a beautiful divider separating the living room from the kitchen. I loved the feel of the deep carvings around the front and the sides of the wood desk, which gave it a touch of class for a lady or that masculine look that a man could appreciate in a design. "Are all the children alright?"

"Yes, Jean, they are all doing fine," she replied.

Her voice began to sound calmer, so I asked, "Did I call at a bad time?"

"No, of course not! How are you doing?"

"We're good. Now, tell me, how is everything with you?"

We talked for a while about her situation at home, and knowing that her heart was broken made me want to cry.

"The apartment across the street is vacant," I said. "Let me call you back when I find out how much it costs per month and how many bedrooms it has." It wasn't long before I reached the office manager and found out the apartment would be ready to rent in two weeks, and I was surprised to find out the first month was free!

I called my sister back to tell her the good news. "Dora, you will be right across the street. Don't worry; everything will work out for you. I love you, Sis, and we'll help you any way we can. We'll talk later."

Dora had done all she could to be a good wife and mom, but people change, feelings change, and then like it or not, you have to make a change too.

The next day, Dora called to let me know she had made a decision. "I've talked to the older children, and they were excited to be moving across the street from you all. So see you in two weeks."

I put the cordless phone back on the base to charge and stopped for a moment to tell the Lord, *Thank you for making a way for Dora and her children. I don't know what's next, Lord, but my faith is in you, and you've never failed us.*

***

Lisa was now a sophomore in high school, and having always been a talkative child, she had no problems when it came to getting acquainted with her classmates. Latrice was now in the fifth grade, and as always, she was eager to learn and meet new people. Sometimes she would bring a classmate home so they could study or hang out and listen to music together in her room. I knew both of them missed their cousins on both sides of the family. They would visit each other often, and sometimes they would have sleepovers with us. My oldest nephew was in the military now, but Dora was sure that when he got out, he would be here to live, at least for a while. Arnetta was having a difficult time dealing with Mama's death, but none of us knew just how hard it was for her until we got a call that made it very clear.

The voice on the other end of the line was shaky. My sister had been crying. She said, "Jean, can I come home?"

I thought that maybe a class had gotten too tough for her and she just couldn't handle the pressure there. I asked, "Is something wrong at school? Bae, tell me what you need us to do." As I sat on the bed beside Ron, I could hear her sobbing.

She asked again, "Can I come home? I can't do this anymore, Jean. I miss Mama so much."

I began to cry with her, and I felt Ron's arm go around my waist as he pulled me over to him. "Give me the phone," he said while taking it from my hand. He answered for me, saying, "Bae, yes, you can come home. As long as we have a roof over our heads, you have a place to stay. Stop crying. It will be alright."

We welcomed every member of our family by giving those who needed help a place to stay until they could get on their feet. Ron's sister, Carmen, served our country for four years and then came to live with us for a very short time while seeking employment. After being on her own, getting an apartment was a priority. She wanted one that was a few blocks from us in the same complex. I was glad she'd decided not to stay in Hawaii because she was like a big sister to Lisa, and I could always count on her to give my daughter good advice. She was one more person in her life encouraging her to finish school and go to college or further her education in the military. The closeness of the Brown family and the Williams family was one that could not be denied.

That closeness became even more apparent as all our siblings started relocating to Indy. It was like a family reunion that was happening gradually, and it made Indy feel more like home.

One day Ron said, "Hey, baby, let's go buy a car!"

Ron had been thinking about it for a while, but each time the subject came up, I very sarcastically said, "Buy a car for what? I'm not letting you drive me anywhere."

"What's the matter? Don't you trust me?" he asked as he tickled me until I slid from the sofa to the floor.

"Yes, I trust you. Now, stop tickling me!"

The girls ran down the hall, and when they got to the living room, they fell on the plush carpet beside me.

"Girls, don't we want a car?" Ron asked.

"Yeah!" they both yelled out.

"What kind? Will it be a big car? What color do we have to get? Can we get a black one?" Lisa asked.

"No, let's get red!" Latrice said.

Ron told them, "We don't need a little car. We have to be comfortable when we hit the road for some weekend trips, and we'll decide the color when we see what they've got, okay?"

The beautiful light blue Cadillac Fleetwood was the only one of its kind on the lot, and Ron just had to leave with the ownership papers in hand. He was so excited about his new purchase that he would just go out to the parking lot, get in his car, and turn the music on. He'd put his head on the headrest and just enjoy having made one more accomplishment in his life as a man . . . no, not a blind man, but a successful man.

"We're going to have it all one day, baby," Ron said as he sat back on the sofa. "Just think; we're off to a good start already." The American dream is to have a wife, a dog, two kids, and a home. "Jean, nothing will get handed to us in life. There are no rich uncles in our family. What about yours?"

"Nope, I can't think of one. We've got each other, and that's all that counts. When all our friends are gone and all our money is spent, we still have each other."

I had learned to read Ron very well and knew that he had a smile on his face. The song "Just the Two of Us" was playing in our bedroom. I thought, *What a perfect song to add to the occasion, and if he needs to be stroked I am certainly willing to rub him the right way any time and any day.*

***

Paul and Pat lived on the west side of town, but Pat and I made sure we kept in touch with each other. "Let's talk to the guys about having lunch one day next week," Pat suggested.

"That sounds good to me, and after lunch we can hang out downtown."

Neither one of us had a job, and there was only so much cleaning and cooking we could do in a day. Pat took on a part-time job, and I decided to volunteer at the Red Cross. We were making stuffed toys for children at Riley Hospital, and finally I was filling my days with something meaningful. Transportation wasn't a problem because the Red Cross had drivers to pick us up and drop us back off at home. We had wonderful conversations every Wednesday, and one lady in particular stood out from the rest. Her name was Francis, but she was affectionately known as Granny. Her sewing skills were very good, so she was never distracted by her conversations with us.

Granny made the hours we volunteered so much fun with discussion topics that covered a wide range, everything from men and how to keep them to politics, religion, and cooking. There was something about her that reminded me of Mrs. Louise from the center. I wasn't sure what it was at first, but then I realized it was her sweet spirit. Her energy just filled the room until it consumed you. Everybody needs someone like Granny in their life. She was full of wisdom and laughter.

Lisa was not adjusting to Indy as well as we thought. The urban environment she had become accustomed to in Gary was very different from Southside Indianapolis, and it was making her life miserable. She loved us all—we knew that for sure—but she wanted to go back home to her familiar surroundings, to her childhood friends, and most of all to her dad.

"Mama, you know I'll write you and call you all the time," she said.

I knew if I tried to speak, the words would get caught in my throat, so I shook my head and just held her for a minute. I hoped she knew that no matter how much distance, there was between us nothing could change my love for her. Seeing her leave was so hard for me to bear. It was as if I were losing a part of myself with no knowledge of how to get it back again. All I kept thinking was, *What am I not doing to keep my family together? Is that so far-fetched that it will never be a reality? Help me get through this, Lord, because if you don't, I know I can't handle this on my own. Maybe moving to Indy was a mistake after all. Latrice will be so lonely without her big sister here to keep her company*, I thought as I stood in front of the patio door listening to the traffic that passed by our apartment.

Once she had made it back to Gary, she called me to let me know she had settled in.

"Mama, please don't think I left because I don't want to be with you. I left because I don't want to live in Indianapolis." She needed to know that everything would be alright and that I wasn't angry with her for leaving, but I replayed that phone call from Lisa in my mind over and over again, for a while. The emotion I felt that was so overwhelming could be summed up in one word: hurt! Although I knew she would be well taken care of with her dad, there was no way I could ever get back the days, months, and years of watching her grow to become the lovely young lady that I knew she would be one day very soon.

"You know you can call me whenever you want, anytime, day or night. It will never be too early or too late. I'll always be here for you, and if you ever want to come back home, you can. I hope you will always believe that your dad, Ron, and I want only what's best for you and your sister. Our love has no limits or boundaries that can't reach your heart." I told her, "I'll always love you, Lisa."

She responded, "I know, and I love you and Ron too, Mama."

I called out to my brother-in-law, Moochie, and asked, "Can you take me to the store today?"

"Sure I can. Just let me know when you're ready," he said.

"I'll be ready in a minute. I just need to get my purse. I'll cook a big pot of chili today if you promise to cook fried fish on Friday," I offered while we were walking to the car.

"Sis, you got yourself a deal if you promise to put me a bowl in the freezer so I can have it for lunch tomorrow at work." I loved his fish as much as he loved my chili, so why not?

"That sounds fair to me," I said as we shook on it. I would just have to fry chicken for Ron, and I knew Latrice would have some of it all. She didn't compete with Ron at the table anymore, but she could still put away a healthy plateful.

It was amazing, Moochie had become as possessive of our car as Ron and really didn't want anyone else to drive it. He would always keep it as clean as possible both inside and out, and whenever he didn't have to show the registration, he would proudly claim the car as his own. Sometimes on the weekend, both he and Ron would be out washing and polishing the Caddie, making it look like it had just been driven off the lot. Moochie would get a couple of cold beers for the both of them to drink, and it was as if they picked up on whatever discussion they were having the last time the car was detailed.

They talked about a few news topics and finally the 40th Street drama, which was on the happening side of town. That was where most of their friends either lived or hung out. It was a fast-paced area to me, and for whatever reason, I didn't fit in with the crowd. Soon Ron was hanging out over there without me.

With the need to fill my unproductive time on my hands, I picked learning grade two braille. I was thinking to myself, *So this is the book that is supposed to be so difficult. Well, I've got nothing but time and plenty of patience.* Jenny, a friend of mine, had told me how important it was to read a little each day to increase my speed. She had often told me it was just like anything else: "If you don't use it, you'll lose it, and you don't want that to happen!"

Jenny was right. This would be a good time to get started and finish up what I should have done a long time ago. Who knows? One day maybe I'd be the one encouraging someone to learn how to read braille so they could enhance their life. I ran my fingers down the page and said, "Lord, whenever the time is right, I want to be prepared for you to use me. I don't know what learning braille has to do with it, but I'm sure you will open the doors I need to enter." *Look out, world! Here I come with my braille book in one hand and my Bible in the other!*

Ron was working hard every day building his business and a name for himself throughout Indy. I don't know if he had a plan to accomplish any particular goal or if he was just going along with the cards that were dealt to him. He always took life one step at a time, or one wave at a time, whichever came first. It didn't matter, as long as he was in motion. He had come to the conclusion that life would not be easy for him as a black man, so whatever he wanted out of life, he would surely have to fight for it. Ron said, "You know I've got the gift of gab. We'll be alright." I never wanted to be up front or in competition with my husband. I just needed to see him reach his full potential. That always made me happy, knowing that he had accomplished his dream in spite of the obstacles he has had to face.

Chapter 15

New Location

We moved to an apartment on the east side of town that seemed nice, but it sure didn't have the amenities at the complex we were leaving. There was a workout room, sauna, pool, tennis court, and clubhouse for the tenants and their guests—all the conveniences a family could want. But with one exception, there were very few children in our neighborhood. "I think Latrice will be happier on this side of town closer to some of her friends. She can walk to school with her classmates and go visit them when she wants. I've been told that it's a pretty safe neighborhood," Ron added.

Ron said there was only one problem; he really didn't sound like he wanted to be at the new apartment. His voice had a quiet, solemn tone to it that sometimes came across as anger, but more often than not it was his concern about a situation that was not completely resolved in his mind as the right choice. He had made the move to make Latrice happy, but after we were all settled in, he finally agreed, "It's not too bad here. You've got everything arranged so nice. Jean, whenever you want, we can move. The lease is only for one year."

I put my arms around his waist and gave him a tight hug. I said, "It's fine for now. Let's just wait and see how things turn out for us here."

Lisa always spent her Christmas school break with us, and each time she came back home, I cooked all her favorite meals, and the three of us enjoyed the holiday visit with her. She was doing well in school and would be graduating soon. I thought to myself, *Oh my gosh, where has the time gone?* I sat at the table to take a short break from cleaning and wrote the menu for Christmas dinner. It was always important to me that I keep the family connected, and what better way to do that than to prepare a feast? After I had typed in braille what seemed to be a pretty complete meal, I turned towards the room Ron and Latrice were in and said, "Alright, you two, tell me if there is anything you want added to this menu. I have ham, chicken, cornish hens, plain dressing, sausage dressing, cranberry sauce, yams, green beans, potato salad, and corn on the cob. For dessert, I'll prepare banana pudding, and you guys can decide what kind of cakes and pies you want. Is there anything else?" I asked. I read the list again quietly to myself.

"Baby, it sounds like you've got everything," Ron replied.

"Yeah, Mama, it all sounds good to me."

"Well, thanks, you two, because I don't want to have to make more than one trip to the store to get everything. Now that I have a menu, I can write down all the ingredients I'll need. Latrice, will you call Lisa and ask her if there is something she really wants me to cook while she's here? And ask her about the desserts too."

"Okay, Mama!" she replied. Latrice was always energetic and happy, but knowing that her sister would be here the next day had her bubbling over with excitement. I loved how they shared little secrets and how Lisa wanted her little sister with her all the time, I wanted them to be close and know they could always depend on each other.

Two days of cooking had gone by, and dinner was to be served at three-thirty. It was a challenge to cook so much in such a small kitchen with so little countertop space, but with the extra table set up in the living room, there were seats for everyone from the youngest to the oldest. We got together and had a ball!

The season changed from the bitter winter that brought us small amounts of snow but lots of icy sidewalks that would have been perfect for ice skating. Young and old alike, attempting to attend school or report to work, were bundled up in their warmest winter coats and boots. It didn't matter where you were in Indy, the main topic of discussion was the weather and how we all wished for warmer days. I guess Ron and I grew up close enough to the Windy City to experience some very inclement weather, so the winters here were mild to us compared to those at home. But eventually all the meteorologists announced that the groundhog had not seen his shadow. We all got our wish quicker than expected; the cool yet sunny days of spring made their arrival more apparent each day. The spring fashions had all the stores slashing the prices of winter clothes, stimulating our minds with beautiful colors, fabrics, and designs for every age and every occasion imaginable.

Just as our surroundings changed, our lives began to make some very significant changes too. Lisa would be graduating this spring and making plans for her future. She hadn't decided if she would go to college or a trade school, but whatever she did, she knew that we would all be there cheering her on. She had so much potential, there was no way she would let anything hold her back.

In the meantime, my baby Latrice would be entering high school that fall. I thought, *I don't know if I'm prepared for the changes that are about to take place, but I'm going to dig my heels in deep and refuse to be moved by all that her teenage years will rapidly bring, with or without our approval.* The two little girls who needed my help for so many things were now young ladies quite capable of making wise choices, and I knew I had to let them. I knew wisdom wasn't a given. They would have to learn from their mistakes. They would have to listen to those who had already traveled the roads they had intentions of venturing down, so they wouldn't make the same mistakes as those who were supposed to be a positive influence in their lives.

Ron seemed to have a schedule that required so much of his day, I often asked him to please pencil me in. "I'd like a little bit of your time too," I said.

His response was usually the same. "I've got to get the IRS off my back, and then I'll slow down."

I thought back to our southside apartment and the man who pounded on our door so hard, he had my heart racing. I'm sure my voice was a little shaky as I shouted out, "Who is it?"

The man on the other side of the door answered me in a tone that made me hesitate for a second, even though my hand was on the doorknob to open it. I froze. He said, "It's the IRS. Is Mr. Brown home?"

"No, he's not home."

He asked, "Are you Mrs. Brown?" There was silence on the other side of the door for a second, and then the booming voice asked, "Will you open the door, Mrs. Brown, so I can give you my card?" He continued with, "Please tell Mr. Brown to call me as soon as possible."

With the security chain still on, I opened the door and reached my hand out to take his card. The man told me that his phone number and office hours were on the card, and he was sorry if he had frightened me. He went on to say he tended to knock a little too hard sometimes.

I said, "That's alright. I'll make sure Ron gets your card as soon as he gets home." I closed the door, leaned my back against it, and listened as he quickly walked across the hall to the stairs.

Ron came home shortly after my phone call to tell him about the visitor we'd had. I met him at the door with a tight hug and probably far more questions then he wanted to answer at the time. "They won't take everything we've worked for, will they?"

Ron said, "Don't you worry about this. I'll call him and work something out with them. I guess that's what happens when you don't get the business training necessary to operate a location. That was my first business," he continued. "How could I have known I would get so far behind in taxes? I'll get them paid, and it will never happen to me again, I can promise you that!"

Ron was rather quiet for the rest of the day, and when he did say something, he expressed just what his feelings were for the almighty IRS.

***

My child cried and sniffled her way through what had to be the most difficult call she ever had to make. She said, "Mama, I'm pregnant. Can I come home?"

"Yes, of course you can come home, Lisa. I'll get someone to drive me there to get you. Stop crying. It will be alright. Get your things packed, and I'll be there this afternoon."

I knew her tears were falling for many reasons, and the number one reason was she felt she had let us down. Her dad had told her,

"You are too young to have a baby. You're a baby yourself!" Wow, eighteen years had gone by so fast. I think he'd forgotten that I was the same age when I got pregnant with her. The only difference was we got married, and that wasn't in the plans for Lisa.

"Listen to me. Your Dad will calm down and spoil that little one just like Ron and I plan to do. Believe me, my child, you are never going to be alone. All of us love you, and we will help you whenever you need it. Your life is just beginning. Decide what you want to do and do it."

God knows what we need and when we need it. I know that because during summer break from school, Latrice called me from her dad's house and said what I had never expected. "Mama, I want to move back home with Daddy. He said if I do, he will let me attend a really good private school! Mama, please let me stay. I'll come and visit you all the time. Please, Mama!"

I sat on the edge of the sofa as I contemplated my response. "Yes, if that's what you want to do, then you can do it."

There was no excitement in my voice when I answered her, and being a child, she asked, "Mama, is everything alright?"

"Yes, baby, everything is alright. I love you so much. I can't wait to see you next week!"

She said, "Thank you. I'll tell Daddy you said yes. I miss you and love you so much, Mama! Tell Ron hello, and I love him too!"

"I'll tell him when he gets home. Talk to you tomorrow. Good night, baby," I said as I pressed the end button to clear the call.

I went to my room and cried myself to sleep. It was a short nap, but when I woke up, I had a different perspective about everything. I wondered if Lisa would come back home to me when she left Gary, and she did. Now we were expecting a healthy granddaughter. I also believed Latrice would come back home too if it was God's will. Her education and determination to be successful would be her driving force that could possibly make her want to relocate to a large city like this, but it would be her love for me that would bring her back to Indy.

Ron called home so excited, I could barely understand what he was saying. There was so much yelling and screaming in the background, I couldn't make it out. "What are you saying?" I asked.

"Jean, we won! We won the World Series of Blind Baseball!"

I had hoped and prayed every year that they would win, and hearing the good news while he was out there on the field made me feel as if I were there. "I'm so glad you won! You just won the 1990 World Series! Congratulations!"

He said, "Jean, the players are opening bottles of champagne all over the field. We did it, baby! We really won! I'll call you when we're on our way home. I love you, Jeannie!"

"I love you too, Ron. What time will you be home? I've got to go and make a special dinner for my champion. Oh yes, tell Booker and Paul congratulations!"

He came home with one more trophy to add to his collection and one more medallion, which he hung around my neck as soon as he came in the house. He had the honor and excitement of playing beep baseball with the Indy Eagles team, where he got the recognition he so greatly deserved. There was no doubt that he loved the accolades, but more than that, he loved the game. Yes, I was one proud wife whether it was victory or defeat. Ron, still full of excitement, continued giving me all the details, saying, "Joe Garagiola attended the game and was there to congratulate the team and shake hands with the players. It was a thrill to have a world-renowned sports reporter from the *Today* show interview me. He asked me how it felt to be a star."

"What did you say?"

"Well, the interview was short, but of course I had to let him know that victory is still sweet even if you're blind," Ron said

***

Moochie, whose smile had touched so many, was now in the hospital in Memphis holding onto every fiber of life. Mom was at his side praying and reading scriptures to him just as she had done for Ron during his hospital stay. It was so hard to believe a group of young men could be so cruel, that they could plan and then follow through with such a merciless act. We were told that their cousin's car had run out of gas, so they walked to a gas station to get a gas can filled. After leaving the station, they were approached by some guys with sticks and chains, and someone had a pipe.

Dear God, I thought, *why would someone assault two men who were out that evening doing nothing more than enjoying each other's company?* The two cousins fought until they couldn't anymore. When they eventually knocked Moochie out, the older guy poured the gasoline on him from the can. The older guy then instructed the youngest boy to light him on fire. The attention of the ruthless young criminals was focused on Moochie, so his and Ron's cousin got away to get help. Without any compassion or concern for Moochie's life, the savage mentality of these young men had created a criminal mind filled with evil thoughts and actions.

The fire spread over Moochie's body, burning through the clothing to his flesh, causing his body to react to the extreme heat. He began running. Thank God for the young lady who saw him from her window and her daughter who called for help. The lady grabbed a blanket and ran from her apartment to tackle what appeared to be a running ball of fire. She didn't know who the stranger was or why he was burning. She only knew that she had to help him. She rolled him on the ground, trying to put out the flame. She knew nothing would alleviate the pain until he could get medical attention, but she stayed right there on the ground with him until help arrived.

"His burns are extremely severe," the doctor said. "We are doing everything in our power to make him as comfortable as possible. You may want to call your family for support. We will allow two visitors at a time but only for a few minutes."

We greeted Mom at the hospital with hugs and let her share as much as she wanted concerning Moochie's condition. She stood up and walked to the doorway of the waiting room and added as an afterthought, "The doctors and nurses have been very nice to me here. They seem to have a really good staff," she said as she looked across the hall to the door to Moochie's room.

I sat on the seat next to Ron, wondering if there was something I could say to comfort him or any of his siblings. It was then that I realized there were no words that could console his mother, his sisters, or his brothers. There was nothing to do but pray to God for his mercy and grace, not just for Moochie but for the entire family, who would need a healing touch.

Mom, with the assistance of a nurse, was preparing to enter Moochie's room. "I'll be out in a few minutes, so whoever wants to go next can get ready."

The doctor announced for all Moochie's visitors to hear, "It is important that we keep his room as sterile as possible, so all visitors must wear a mask, bonnet, gown, shoe covers, and gloves. It will be very easy for him to get an infection, and we can't risk that. I'll look in on him first thing in the morning. He'll be more hydrated then, and I'll be able to tell you more about his condition." The doctor stepped away, briefly acknowledging one of the nurses, then stopped, turned to look at Mom, and told her in a more sympathetic voice, "Please get some rest. We'll take good care of him."

The hours soon became days as our hope increased for Moochie's life to continue. The next couple of weeks were filled with an unequal balance of emotions. Ron, who was never at a loss for words, was consumed with so much anger and helplessness at the same time. "Those no-good bastards should not have been given life when all they were going to do is end my brother's life! Jean, what if he doesn't make it? Hasn't my mother been through enough?"

I tried to offer him some reassurance. I told him, "Yes, she has, but don't give up just yet, Ron."

There was a fear in my heart because of the hatred Ron had expressed for the men. That hatred made me wonder if he could commit a crime that would put him on the same level as those lowlifes. He told me one night, "If I could get my hands on them, if I could get revenge for what they did to my brother, I would be alright! Jail isn't good enough for them. I want them to suffer just like Moochie is suffering now!" He went on to say, "Aw, what the hell. I want every one of them dead, and their mamas too for bringing them into this world!"

Moochie's life expired a few days later, and what had horrified the whole family had come to an end. "Those young punks all deserve to die!" Ron said. His heart was now filled with rage. God's love would have to intervene to change his heart, or his soul would be lost forever.

There is a time and a season for all things, and tomorrow is not promised to any of us, I thought as we were getting dressed the morning of the funeral. Ron was quiet all morning, and I wondered if he was thinking back on the days when he and Moochie were growing up. Was he reflecting on the day when he was shot? Maybe he was thinking about the ride to my house for the first time and how he had devised a plan that would determine if he would make the visit a short one or not. Perhaps he was thinking about the day he went to buy his first car and Moochie took it for a spin. *Lord, I don't know what his thoughts are on this day, but I hope they are good ones*, I thought.

Ron and Moochie had partied together, and often I would hear them joking around and jiving with each other. Their laughter was contagious, and I was glad that I had been a part of the joy and happiness they shared. I grieved the loss of my brother-in-law, who was so kind and loving. The memories of his life with us will always remain in my heart.

I started walking towards Ron and asked, "Are you ready?"

"Yeah, as ready as I can be," he replied.

I stopped to give him a hug and said, "I love you." As usual, I reached up to make sure his tie was straight. It was straight most of the time, but just in case it wasn't, I wanted him to know. I got him down to the smallest detail.

"I love you too," he said as he gave me kisses on my forehead and a long affectionate hug.

With all the family and friends there to share comforting words after the service, I believed the Brown family had made it through one more tragedy with God's help. Some laughed as they reminisced about Moochie's childhood while others talked about the more recent years they had spent with him and how much he would be missed.

I thought about my grandfather. When Mama died, he had said, "A mother or father should never have to bury their child." Like Mama, Moochie was an adult with a child of his own, but he was still one of Myra Brown's children.

God had chosen to take him home but not before Moochie had gotten a chance to tell her that he had given his life to Jesus. "I know he's home with the Lord," Mom said to us all. "I knew he and I would both be alright after that conversation."

Chapter 16

Harmony?

The morning nausea that came along with pregnancy lasted beyond morning for the first months. Lisa had always been a picky eater and craved shrimp at the time, but the little one inside her didn't want seafood or many of the mother's other food choices, it seemed. Five minutes later, the meal would have Lisa in the bathroom pleading for relief and begging God to make the vomiting stop. After a while, she could finally eat almost anything her little heart desired, and she did.

Eventually the waiting was over, and we were all excited to meet the new addition to our family. It had been a long nine months, but our healthy granddaughter was born. I was amazed at how fast my daughter's motherly instincts kicked in.

"Ron, it's a girl!" I exclaimed. "A beautiful, healthy baby girl!"

"How is Lisa?"

"Lisa is doing fine. She just needs to get some rest," I replied.

"Is the baby in the room now? What's her name?" Ron had so many questions, and I thoroughly enjoyed his excitement.

"Yes," I replied. "And her name is Jasmine Latrice." I didn't want to leave Ron by himself in the waiting room, but I knew he would be fine. I went back into Lisa's room, where Latrice was holding her little niece.

The nurse came back in to check Lisa's vitals to make sure everything was alright with our baby. When the nurse left, we gathered our belongings and told the new mom to get some rest while baby Jasmine was sleeping. We made sure not to make too much noise and disturb the little one, but we left Lisa with promises of returning the next day.

***

Jasmine brought an extra sense of joy to our home. Having a new baby in the house made it feel more serene. I began to recognize that the steps we took were being ordered by God to make our lives gel according to His plan. I also acknowledged the distance that now existed between Ron and me, and I desperately wished for the words to say to break the ice or at lease warm the chill.

We were preparing for another move since the lease was almost up. I was packing some of the things that we didn't need immediately, when the sound of the phone ringing made me stop wrapping the vase that was on the end table. Being careful not to drop it, I rushed to put tape on the bubble wrap, and then I reached with my left hand to grab the phone.

"Hello?"

"Hey, baby, I won't be coming right in from work, but I won't be out too late," Ron's voice said at the end of the line, getting right to the point.

No surprise, I thought to myself.

"Are you still there?" Ron asked.

"Yes, I am," I replied, barely keeping the disappointment out of my voice. It was a Friday night, and lately it was a shock when I didn't get that call letting me know he was going to be out longer. "I'll see you when you get here," I finally said. I didn't know where he was going or who he would be with, but I did know for sure that something was eating away at him, and I was the one feeling the bite. I didn't know what to do, but I knew that giving up was not an option.

"I'm just going to hang out with the fellas for a while," he continued in his most convincing voice. "I'll be home before it's too late."

"Yeah, I know," I replied dryly. "I'll see you when you get home."

I didn't want to hear him say again, "If you want to go out, get up and go. I'm not making you stay at home. Just like you go to church, you can go anywhere else you want to go. I'm a grown man, and I'll go wherever I want when I want." I was starting to toughen up just a little, so his words didn't have quite the same effect as they did the first time. I hung up the phone and went to check the locks on the doors, praying, *Lord, tell me what to do.*

The hours seemed to pass by quickly with Jazzy in the house. *You're such a good baby*, I thought to myself as I stood in the doorway for a second, listening for her little sounds. I'd hear her make that little cooing noise she made when she woke up, that is, if she didn't nasty her diaper, because in that case, there would be a loud cry for sure since she couldn't stand to have poop on her bottom.

Now I understand why Mama had that proud look on her face when she talked about any of her grandchildren. Being grandparents was pretty cool, and we were loving every minute of it! There were many times when Jasmine would wake up, and Ron would proudly say, "Jean, go get her for me. You know I can put her right back to sleep in no time."

I would grab a Pamper, whisper to Lisa, "I've got her," and take the baby to our room, where Ron would lay her on his chest. She would sleep there for hours while Ron flipped through the television channels searching for something worth watching.

By spring, it was time to move, and it was so nice to be living in a house again. Although all of the apartments we'd lived in had something nice to offer, this was our first house together. I was excited to decorate and plan family dinners for us. Ron was happy just to have more space. He kept talking about how the place was large enough to have nice summer get-togethers and have some of the fellas over to play cards sometimes.

"Yes, that would be nice," I replied thoughtfully, but the truth was that as long as he was there, it didn't matter because I was happy with him. However, lately, no matter what the celebration was for, I never really felt included. Smoking and drinking didn't have to be a part of socializing for me to have a good time with the company I was with, but that seemed to be the whole purpose of Ron and his friends getting together. *Life has to have more to offer than what we are experiencing right now*, I thought to myself.

I began to wonder if I was expecting too much from Ron. *Maybe it's not his lifestyle but mine that needs a complete makeover*, I thought. I was starting to spend more time in prayer and a lot less time in places where

I found myself in totally uncomfortable situations. Lately, sometimes the uncomfortable place even included our home.

Lisa found a job, and I kept Jasmine so she wouldn't have to find a sitter for her. The thought of the baby having to go to some stranger's house would have been more than either one of us wanted to deal with, especially at such a young age.

"You know, they don't stay babies for long," I told Lisa while she was making plans to take Jasmine to her dad's house in the summer for a few weeks. Her dad and Latrice wanted to bond with the newest member of the family, and they were just a couple of hours away. They were getting prepared for little Jasmine's arrival and made sure all the necessities were there for her. A cabinet in the kitchen had been filled with a variety of jars and boxes of baby food, some extra bottles, and plenty of formula to last the entire summer and then some.

It was wonderful to hear the excitement in Latrice's voice when she called home to tell me what they did each day. She talked about how she loved taking Jasmine to visit family and her friends from home. We always ended our phone calls with Latrice reminding me of how much she loved and missed me, and how she was so excited to be with us for the holidays. Her phone calls always put me in a better mood.

The months passed by quickly, and by the time Thanksgiving Day arrived, Jasmine was nine months old and able to enjoy her first holiday dinner at our table. It made us all laugh when she put her little hand on the plate and grabbed a handful of sweet potatoes. Ron and Lisa both said that she would no longer want anything from a jar again.

Jasmine was starting to walk then, taking a few steps without holding onto anything; then she would plop down on the floor and start crawling again. A few weeks went by, and she let go of the pillow on the sofa and walked across the room. We could hear her coming because of the sound of the little bells on her shoestrings, so we began to clap for her. In all the excitement she burst out in laughter. With her arms outstretched, she made it across the room to the love seat.

"Well," Ron said "let's see how happy you all will be when those little fingers start getting into everything. You're going to have to either pack all the cute things up that are on the tables or keep a broom and dustpan handy."

"Tell me," I asked, "did you ever see Mom moving everything from her tables, or did she just move the child?" I immediately left the room after giving him something to think about, telling him what my mom had often said to me: *"Kids will be kids."*

***

The National Federation of the Blind became more important to me than I had ever imagined. I was hearing more and more about legal cases that involved discrimination. Blind people were being challenged on jobs they had worked at for years as a sighted person. It was simply devastating. Because they had lost their sight, employers felt they could no longer perform their job duties. It didn't matter to the employers who terminated the employees; it was as if they thought that being blind meant the employee had no obligations or responsibilities. The more our organization fought to have society accept us for who we are, the more they tried to stand their ground.

"Yes, we are blind and we have limitations, but we will stand up and fight for our right to be treated equally." Dr. Marc Maurer had been elected as our national president several years before, and he had been groomed by the best, Dr. Kenneth Jernigan. Dr. Maurer ruled "the movement" with an iron fist and was dedicated to the cause. The leaders of our organization were second to none. Yes indeed, it was true; we were the voice of the nation's blind. "We will not capitulate in our battle. Just as Dr. King fought for our civil rights as black people to have equality, the National Federation of the Blind will stand in solidarity against anything that is a threat to our rights as blind individuals."

I looked over my braille fundraising notes and began to wonder if things would ever get better for the blind people of our generation. Lisa and Latrice hadn't developed retinitis pigmentosa, but if they had, like all moms, I would want them to have every opportunity to advance that sighted children are given. I was so thankful for the leaders, our members, and those who supported our efforts because without them, none of our accomplishments would have been possible.

When it was time to run for office, Ron was selected as our state president. I knew he would do the very best he could to build our affiliate organization. I was once again proud of his accomplishments and his dedication to the organization.

***

While Ron and I were keeping busy with our local chapter, Lisa was trying to find her way in life and thought she might want to become a hairstylist. She styled her hair and anyone else's who would let her. She tried it all, from coloring and cutting to braiding hairstyles. The more practice she got, the better each style looked. But once she enrolled in school, her desire to become a hair stylist soon vanished. "Mama, being a hairstylist is not what I want to do. I can't see myself getting up every day for the next thirty years styling hair all day."

"Don't worry, Lisa; you'll figure it out, and when you do, you'll do a fantastic job at whatever it is." Giving her a smile, I added, "Sometimes it takes a little time to figure out what we want to do in life. Just be patient. Everything happens in God's time, Lisa." I didn't want her to work just any old job and be miserable. I wanted her to search her heart and find something she was passionate about.

Months later, Lisa sat us down again and told us she had some news to share. Neither one of the girls was ever good at keeping secrets or at sugarcoating anything, so Lisa kept her announcement direct and to the point. "Ron, Mama, I went to the doctor today, and he confirmed what I thought already. I'm pregnant. It's a boy."

"So we're going to have a grandson. How many months are you?" I asked.

"I'm four months, Mama," Lisa answered as she moved her keys and key ring around on the glass tabletop. I was surprised, but nevertheless we were going to have our first grandson, and he would arrive in May.

"Well, Jasmine, you're going to have a baby brother," I said as I picked her up and bounced her on my lap.

Ron, the man of many words, simply said, "A grandson. It will be nice to have a boy in the house."

***

Ron's new job as a peer counselor kept him occupied, and I was very impressed with the success he had finding work for people living with a disability. I knew it gave him a great sense of pleasure. He made a significant difference in his clients' lives by giving them confidence and hope they had never experienced before.

I wondered if Ron knew the reason for his blindness. Surely God knew he would be someone who would serve others, that he would, despite his blindness, be showing them the way to a brighter future. Ron never would have become the man that he was if he had continued to travel down the path that led him only to trouble as a sighted teen. Many days I prayed to God to help him understand that if he would only hold on to his integrity, God would open doors for him that he never dreamed of entering.

Latrice was a junior in high school now, and I was so proud of her. She had grown up to be quite a young lady.

"Mama, I'm going to attend college when I graduate next spring. I know I can do it, but I get so nervous just thinking about it! I'm going to make you so proud of me," she said.

I thought back to her second-grade class, the day she sat at her little desk with her head on both her arms, covering them with tears. The teacher told me when I entered the room how upset she was because she had a B on her report card.

I walked across the room and kneeled down beside her chair. "Baby girl, as long as you did your best, there is nothing to cry about." I took some tissue from my purse and dried her little face. "I love you this much," I said as I stretched out my arms for her to fall into.

"I love you too, Mama," she replied.

I took her hand and said, "Let's go home!"

We talked and laughed all the way, and by the time she had changed her school clothes, my ambitious child was already telling me how one day she was going to be a business lady.

I didn't know when or where, but I believed that one day she would see her dream come true. From time to time she would work as a front office assistant at her dad's family business. There was no doubt that working and spending time there had given both the girls valuable business skills. They had a close relationship with their dad's side of the family, but spending time at work with them made it even stronger.

The girls had one aunt who loved them as much as I did her two children; and one uncle who simply adored his nieces. Divorce is never simple; it's always complicated. Divorcing a spouse also means divorcing his family and all the friends you thought you had together. Well, there's one thing I know for sure; I never want to go through that again. I don't see Ron's sisters or his brother all the time, but I don't know what I would do if I couldn't visit with them again at all and share some good times together.

"What do you want to do for your birthday, Ron?" I asked one afternoon.

"Well, let's see." He hesitated for a moment and then said, "The weather is going to be really nice tomorrow. How about grilling out and inviting some of the family and a few friends over? That is, if you feel up to making the sides for me."

"Of course I will," I responded. "You probably need to call our cousin Marshall, though, to see if he will grill for you. If not, I'm sure Lisa will help you get it started; that is, if she doesn't go into labor."

The next day, we were in party mode. "Mama, what do you need help with?" Lisa asked. She was up and ready to get the ball rolling. "I've got the list of things you want from the store. I'm going to pick up my cousin Shonda so she can help me, and I'll be right back." She was walking to the door when she stopped and asked, "Are you sure this is all you need?"

"Yes, I'm sure. Thank you!"

"Lisa had better slow down or she's going to have that baby early," Ron said after she had shut the front door. "Look at how big she is. I mean, her belly is huge!"

"Oh, don't worry. He won't come until it's time. She'll be fine."

Marshall came prepared to grill all the meats and make his sauce that everyone loved. The party went on for hours, and Ron certainly enjoyed it.

No sooner had everything been cleaned up, everyone had gone home, and we had gone to bed, than Lisa woke us up, crying about contractions. We hurried to get dressed and called for her cousin Margret to take us to the hospital. Ron would stay home with Jasmine, and I gave him a quick rundown of where all the bottles, milk, and wipes were. "Listen, if you need to know something else, just call me."

I called, "Lisa, are you ready?"

No sooner had I asked the question than I heard her cousins laughing so hard because Lisa was trying to eat another piece of rib before she left the house.

I went to the kitchen doorway. "Girl, wash your greasy hands and come on! You are not going to have that baby in this house!" I exclaimed.

We piled into the car, and Margret did her best to stay within the speed limit as we made our way to the hospital. Thankfully, no babies were born on her back seat.

Margret and I had settled into the birthing room, and it wasn't long before a nurse came to update us. "She's dilated to six centimeters already. It shouldn't be too much longer before the doctor will be in, and we'll introduce this little one to his family." She turned to Lisa and instructed her to breathe slow and easy during contractions.

I stood on one side of the bed, and Margret was on the other, holding her hand. We were praying and giving Lisa the cup of ice chips that she crunched on to wet her parched mouth in between the labor pains. The nurse returned to check on her progress, and with much excitement in her voice, she said, "I'm going to page the doctor now, and you will be holding your baby shortly!"

I heard the sound of water running and knew the doctor was scrubbing his hands. A few seconds later, he was putting on latex gloves. He took a few quick steps and was at the bed, talking to Lisa in a calm voice while all the time giving her instructions. Finally, after a few very hard pushes by Lisa, the doctor delivered our first grandson!

I took my phone out of my purse to call Ron while the nurse was cleaning the baby and the doctor was making sure Lisa was alright. "Ron," I said excitedly, "Courdney was born a few minutes ago, and both mother and son are doing fine."

Ron had his hands full with his two-year-old granddaughter while we were at the hospital, and what a laugh he got. When he changed her diaper, he got ready to put the new one under her, and she was watching his every move. "This way, Paw Paw," she said as she took the Pamper from him, turned it the right way, laid down on it, and waited for him to fasten the tabs. We all knew Jasmine was smart and that she was ready to be potty-trained. Besides, buying Pampers for two would get to be pretty expensive.

Latrice came home to visit two days after her nephew was born, and the jealousy that arose in little Jasmine was so funny. She would stretch her arms out for Latrice to pick her up when she saw her rocking Courdney to sleep. Sometimes she would just try to hold Latrice's hands, anything that would take attention from the baby. Latrice would say, "I'll get her in a minute, Mama. She has to learn to share her Tee-Tee now. Jasmine, come sit on the sofa next to me and your little brother. You know I love you, and as soon as I put the baby to bed, we can do whatever you want to do."

Jasmine would nod her little head and respond, "Okay, Tee-Tee," and from the excitement in her voice, you could tell everything was alright in her little world.

Chapter 17

Searching

Sometimes it's good to get in a quiet place where there is nothing to interrupt your thoughts except the Holy Spirit. The party going on in the basement was loud. I often wondered why our neighbors didn't knock on our door and request that the music be turned down.

Their party was going strong, and the music was blasting. The smoke seeped up through the vents, forcing its nasty taste and smell into my nose and my lungs. *This has got to be hell*, I thought. I was irritated by just the very thought of cancer from a cigarette that someone else found pleasure in smoking.

I closed the bedroom door, went over to the triple-drawer dresser, and opened the small door that gave me access to my three small lingerie drawers. I took out my sexy little black teddy lingerie, slipped it on, got in bed, and pulled the top sheet over me as if it were my blanket that I carried everywhere when I was a toddler. *Peace*, I thought to myself as I settled my head on my pillow and said in almost a whisper, "God, where is the peace you promised you would give if my mind stayed on you?" I lay there waiting to get an answer in all the noise. All I wanted was a few minutes of peace and quiet around me until I could fall asleep.

There was no voice to identify, not even the sound of someone breathing, but I felt a presence there with me. If someone had come in, I would have heard the old silver doorknob being turned; I would have heard the sound of the old hinges squeaking as they always did when we opened the door; but there was no sound, none at all.

The beat of my heart sped up just a little when I felt the other side of the bed sink down as if someone were there, but I didn't feel afraid when I swiped my hand over the bed and felt absolutely nothing. It was in that moment of calmness, with my hands outstretched, that I found the peace inside me that could be called perfect peace. I immediately fell asleep . . . not a restless sleep, but a peaceful sleep until the next morning.

I've heard so often that it is extremely difficult to find employment as a blind person, but I was depending on God to show me favor. *I'll discuss it with Ron and get a feel for his thoughts about me finding work, and everything will happen just as it's supposed to.* I put on my robe and slippers and went to the dining room, where Ron was sitting, sipping on a cup of coffee while listening to the television.

"Good morning," I said as I approached the back of his chair. I leaned over the top of his head and gave him a kiss on the forehead.

He replied, "Good morning to you, Mrs. Brown!"

"I thought you would have slept in a little longer, but you're up early," I said.

"Well, if you're going to hoot with the owls at night, you got to be able to soar with the eagles in the morning," he replied.

"True, but does this eagle know that it's Saturday? There's no need to rise at the crack of dawn."

Ron laughed as he got up, telling me, "Have a seat, my love. I'll pour you a cup of coffee."

"Thank you, honey!" I replied eagerly. "Ron, I've been thinking of finding a job. What do you think?"

"I think you should if you want to," he said after a moment.

"I do, and I'm going to make some calls first thing Monday morning."

The temp service was more than willing to help me find employment, and they accomplished their task in less than two weeks. "Yes, I can report to work on Tuesday at four-thirty a.m." I said, as I reached for my braille writer already loaded with a sheet of paper. I took down the name of the company, address, phone number, and supervisor I would report to before my shift started at five o'clock.

The service representative said, "Well, Mrs. Brown, congratulations. You'll work four days this week, but next week you will get your full forty hours and a chance to get some overtime if you want. Call me if you have any questions. If you have to be off work, let me know as much in advance as possible so I can contact your supervisor until your trial period is up."

"Thank you for all your help, and I'll talk to you soon!" I couldn't wait to hang up the phone so I could let out a loud scream of joy. "Finally, I've got a job! Yes! Thank you, Jesus!!"

I was filled with so much excitement when Ron came home from work, I met him at the door. "Hi, Ron. Guess what!" I said as I threw my arms around him.

Teasing me as he so often did, he said, "Well, let me see; I'll bet you won the lottery."

"No!" I said with a laugh.

"Then my next guess would be that you now have a job."

"Yes!"

"I knew that's what it had to be, come on in the room with me while I put my work bag away, and you can tell me all about it."

I could tell that he was happy for me because he kept saying, "My Jeannie's got a job. You go, girl!" I loved it when I could picture Ron smiling at me. Whenever I made him happy, the joy it brought to me was indescribable.

I went on to tell him, "Working will be good for me. Whatever the job is, I'll make the best of it. Terri is going to take me to work until I can find a permanent ride, and she said Lorenzo can pick me up in the afternoon. In the event those two can't take me, there's got to be someone who lives on this side of town who's going that way." My mind was racing. After I had blurted out all that, I paused to take a deep breath.

"Don't worry, Jean; you'll find a way to get to work. At least you've got it figured out for a couple of weeks. Jean, what would have been bad is if you had gotten the job and couldn't be there on your start date," he said

"You're so right," I said. "Come on, let's go eat. There's a pot of ham hocks and pinto beans, fried chicken, and corn bread ready for dinner."

"Then I'm on my way."

I walked in about ten minutes early to work and found a line that I was told to stand in. Everyone was waiting for instructions from the supervisor. "I heard they'll put us wherever we're needed," I could hear a lady about three or four people ahead saying.

A guy behind me was holding a conversation with his friends, and I heard him refer to me, saying, "Oh, how nice. They even hire people who have a disability."

"Oh, I wouldn't mind showing her around," another guy said in a lewd voice.

The other guy with him seemed to be a little bit embarrassed and said, "It's too early to be talking like that, and you ought to show some respect."

I didn't say a word as I waited in the long line, but I did turn in the direction of his voice and gave him a smile.

Finally, the supervisor was there. I thought to myself, *I guess we will be shown to our line now.*

There was no doubt that the supervisor was in charge. He ordered, "Each position has a number, so step up if I call your number, and you'll be told your job duties. I need group one over here, group two can go over by the ropes, and group three can line up along this wall."

I was standing there alone when he walked up to me and said, "I don't know what I'm going to do with you just yet, so just take about four steps to your left and stay there until I come back for you."

He turned to walk away when I asked him, "Aren't I supposed to be packing?"

He kept walking as he answered me, saying, "I don't know." He sounded angry, but so was I, mainly because there were several names called from that list who did not even show. I stood there leaning against the brick wall for the next thirty-five minutes. Everyone who passed by me asked in a concerned tone, "Are you waiting for someone, or can I walk with you to the break room so you can sit down?"

I decided to take matters in my own hands. They had accepted my application, and now that I was there, they didn't know what to do with me. Ron had always told me that when an employer doesn't know what you are capable of, then you have to be assertive enough to show them. *Jean, the ball is in your court, so show them what you're working with.* I had listened to the doors closing on the right-hand side of the room and was convinced that the office was in that area. I took my cane and started in that direction. I heard the sewing machines and the sound of conveyer belts running, and I managed to get past all of it.

Suddenly someone was coming towards me. "Excuse me, where are you going? I'm the line leader for this area," she explained, rushing over to see if she could assist me.

"Is the office right over there?" I asked.

"Yes," she said. "I'll walk with you. Are you here to see someone?"

"I've been waiting for approximately forty-five minutes now to find out where I'll be working. I'm sure that all the new hires are already on the clock. So if you can direct me to the correct person, I would greatly appreciate it."

I didn't know that a supervisor had walked up and was listening to us until he asked, "Are you Jean Brown?"

"Yes, I am," I replied.

"I'm Ed, and she's Paige. You'll work on her line, and your duties are to inspect, cut all loose threads, and pack them on a skid. If you know someone who can give you a tour of the plant, let me know and I'll approve it for you."

"Thank you, Ed," I said. "Actually, I do know someone, and if tomorrow is not too soon, I would love to have a tour and mobility lesson."

The following morning, Ron went to work with me, and with cane in hand, he led the way, showing me the layout of the plant. I walked with him to the office, to the break room, to the line, and then to the ladies' room. I never could understand how he could walk into a building that he had never been in and seem so sure of himself. He taught me by saying, "Listen to the sounds around you, Jean, and don't be afraid to touch things that are stationary with your cane. We'll walk through it a few times until you are comfortable, and just know that you can always ask your coworkers if you get confused. We'll take a look at the time clock before I leave and see where your time card needs to go."

I was so thankful my husband was a take-charge kind of guy. At times, I felt lost without him by my side. Ron took me by the hand and told me, "I'll see you when you get home from work, and I'll have your bubble bath ready for you."

Before long, work was over, and I was ready to get home to my promised bubble bath. I walked in to the sound of a smooth jazz CD. I took a hot, relaxing bath as I told Ron about my day.

"I bought dinner. Do you want to eat now or relax for a while?"

"I think I would like to unwind for a while," I told Ron as I slipped on something comfortable.

We held each other for a while, and as he leaned forward to kiss me on the neck, I thought, *He knows just how to please me, and nothing means more to me than keeping this man satisfied.*

I heard him whisper softly, "Just relax, baby. I got you."

Lisa had been working for Ron as his assistant for several months now and had met a young man named Jerry who worked in the post office. I think it's safe to say they were attracted to each other; his name kept popping up in her conversations. Yes, more and more, we heard about Jerry and knew there was something special about the relationship. Lisa seemed to perk up when she talked about him, and it became very clear that she was definitely falling in love. It wasn't long before Jerry asked for her hand in marriage, and we were all thrilled to have him and his two children be a part of the family.

On January third, my oldest daughter and Jerry were married. My prayer was that they would share a bond that would keep them united for all time. My oh my, what a day! Lisa's little family gathering was at our home, where we had wedding cake and a few trays of finger foods. Ron turned the television on to the cartoon channel for Jasmine and Courdney while I put away the leftovers. As I stood at the kitchen sink washing the trays, I pictured my beautiful daughter with her handsome husband exchanging their vows, their rings, and their love for each other. It had been a beautiful wedding that filled my heart with so much happiness for them.

We had occupied the little stone-front house for almost three years. Packing was a real chore, but I couldn't wait to relocate. *What a joy it will be to leave these four walls. There is just no room for every piece of baggage, so I'll leave the bad memories and move out with only what has made a lasting impression in my heart.*

I thought about the visits Latrice had made so she could spend some time with her family here in Indy, which was always nice. All the fun we had together before Lisa started living in her own apartment added to the special memories too. It was here that I had babysat my grandchildren, watched them take their first steps, and say their first words. They had helped to keep me busy, and I sat thinking about how fascinated I'd been with having the chance to spend so much time with them. There was nothing like watching them grow up and having them be a part of my life as much as possible.

The visit from Aunt Lee for the Easter holiday made me remember how blessed our lives were to have her in it. That week while she was with us, I spent the entire time enjoying all the love and wisdom she always gave, just as I did when I was a child. I also reflected on the fun we all had with Mike here in this house when he moved to Indy and lived with us until he was ready to settle into his own apartment. It was in this house that Arthur saw a small part of his dream come true when he entered a poetry contest and was named the poet of the year. His poem "Flowers for No Reason" was published in *A Sea of Treasures*, and he vowed to one day be known as a poet. We all reassured him that he could do anything he believed he could do.

The move to our new house took place during the spring. This time we were moving next door to someone who had been a true friend for years. James was employed at a branch of the post office that was located in the same area as Ron's vending location. He was a hard worker and friendly to everyone he met. Ron rode in to work with him every day, and he made himself available to assist us in any way he could. James later married a fellow postal employee after dating her for a while. Although we were neighbors, neither one of us did a lot of visiting. She was a newlywed, and I kept to myself most of the time unless I was working.

On occasion, she and I would visit with each other standing on her lawn or one of our front porches. It was evident that she had talked to her husband and encouraged him to reach out to me. One day he called the house one day and said, "Mrs. Brown, let me know if you ever need to go shopping or get dropped off anywhere. I'm available to take you. It can be a doctor's appointment or grocery shopping. Just let me know, okay?"

James seemed a bit nervous, but nevertheless he was a polite young man, and that won me over. "I sure will. Thank you," I replied.

Ron and I had discussed time and time again how difficult it was to get around without a driver. This is no small town, and he or I often needed a ride. Depending on a cab daily would cost a small fortune. Of course, there was the shared ride plan, which was fine for doctor visits, but it was always iffy depending on whether you made your appointment on time. At times, you could easily be stuck with no return ride home.

Talking to Ron, I said with a chuckle, "It will cost a little more, but I've been told he's a careful driver and very punctual. I can't ask for more than that."

Ron's voice was filled with excitement when he said, "Jean, I just called one of the NFB centers and talked with them about a master's program teaching cane travel. It's a new program, and I'm the first one to sign up. It's in Rustin, Louisiana, and I can be finished in two years!"

It wasn't that I couldn't believe my ears on the other end of the phone, but I was shocked at the enthusiasm in his voice. How could he be so thrilled to pack up and be gone from home for months at a time? The more he talked about it, I began to realize how important it was to him.

"I'll come home every quarter. You know I have to be present at the vending location or my business counselor won't be happy. I can turn the business over to you while I'm gone. I know you can handle it for me, if you will?"

"Of course I will," I replied. "Listen, Ron, you don't have to worry about anything here. Just get that degree and hurry back home. I'm going to miss you so much," I said softly.

He said, "I'll miss you too, but I'm trying to make things better for us. Just hang in there with me and you'll see."

I packed Ron's luggage and checked it a few times to make sure I didn't leave out his favorite shirt or anything that he might need while he was away. Finally, the day arrived for Ron to catch his flight. I went through the entire morning dreading the clock announcing the eleven o'clock hour.

While preparing the last little bit for his journey, Ron said, "I'll call you at the airport while I'm waiting for my connecting flight."

"I'll be right here waiting for your call," I said. As we hugged each other tight, I told him, "I love you so much, Ron."

"I know, but I love you more," he replied. "Come on, Jeannie; walk me to the door," he said.

Ron went across the porch with a carry-on bag on his shoulder and his largest suitcase on wheels. He pulled it to the cab. The driver met him at the back of the car, offering to put his luggage in the trunk. We exchanged one more hug and kiss goodbye, and a moment later, the cab pulled off, taking a piece of my heart with it. Instantly I felt the overwhelming loneliness begin to take over. I knew for certain that without my Ron, nothing was going to be the same here.

I received a call from Ron as soon as he made it to Louisiana. "Jeannie, I'm here. I'm in Rustin!" Every word rang out with such excitement, I couldn't help but grab a hold of his happiness and go along for the ride.

"I'm so glad you made it there safe."

"Oh yeah. Now I've got to get familiar with my surroundings."

"Oh Lord, look out, Rustin. Ron Brown is in town," I said.

"Hey, what does that mean?" he said.

"Well, it wasn't me who started calling you the party animal."

He said, "Naw, it's all about the books this time around. I had to go away so I could stay focused. Anyway, time will go by fast, and I'll be back at home getting on your nerves again."

"It's okay. I don't know what to do when you aren't here to irritate me. Besides, you do it so well, no one could ever replace you," I told him.

I could hear the smile in his voice. "Thank you, Mrs. Brown. That means a lot."

These few weeks were the hardest for me, but I kept myself busy most days, and from the conversations with Ron, it was clear he did the same. I continued to bowl on our fall Indy Blind Bowling League every Wednesday, and it was good to still see our friends. Bowling was never my strong point, but the conversations were always good.

Ron was still the state president for the National Federation of the Blind. Although he was miles away in Rustin, he wanted to stay abreast of everything that was happening in the affiliate at all times. Pam, our second vice president, and I kept him well informed, so he never had to feel like he was out of the loop. I gave him the banking totals each day and reassured him that the orders had been placed for the vending machine products for the week. There was always something to do, from filling to fixing the machines. It seemed that every day in the vending business, there was a situation to resolve, and due to all the free time I would have had on my hands, I was more than happy to be working there.

"Hi, Ron. Did you get my voice message?" I asked tearfully into the receiver.

"No, I didn't," he said. "What's wrong. Are you crying?"

I began to explain the awful housing situation that had occurred while he was away. "We have two months to find someplace else to live, Ron. She's not going to let us buy the house."

"Alright, Jeannie, stop crying. Here's what I need you to do. Whenever you can get a ride, go look at some apartments. Don't worry; get as much packed as you can, and I'll come home and get us moved."

"I really liked it here," I said as I wiped my face and plopped down on the sofa. "It was just a conversation with her. We have nothing in writing."

"That was our fault, baby. We should have gotten an agreement that stated we would purchase the property at the end of our second year here," Ron said. "Don't worry; it won't happen again." I could hear the frustration in his voice as he spoke.

When I hung up the phone, I slowly walked around in each room, returned to the living room, and murmured to myself, "If I bring some boxes home each day, I can have this done and be ready to go when Ron gets home."

It took about three weeks to find an apartment, but when I did, the walk-through with my nephew's wife, Tonya, and the manager of the complex, we both loved it. I couldn't wait to tell Ron how nice it was, and it was in our price range.

"Aunt Jean, come take a look at this patio, and if you walk up the two steps to your left, that's where the trash bin is," Tonya said as she went out the sliding glass door.

Using my cane, I followed her out to the patio to check out its length and width. "I really like it, and I'm sure Ron will. We can put our grill right over there," I said as I tapped my cane tip on the concrete to the left of the glass door. I turned to the manager and told her, "Thank you for your patience, and I hope everything will be approved."

"Thank you for coming in, and from the looks of things, I should be able to let you know today. I'll call you," she said as we went out the door to the left.

It had been a long day at the post office, but now my heart was filled with anticipation. *Oh, this one just has to be the one for us!* I got another empty box from the pile and began to tape the bottom of it. *There are so many CDs to be packed, but before I start, I've got to take out Smokey because I work the best to his music.* The CD began to play, and I stood there for a minute lost in my own thoughts. I moved on to the kitchen to start packing cookware that I wouldn't need immediately, and then the phone rang.

"Hello, Jean. This is Barb calling to let you know that you and your husband got approved for the apartment."

"Oh my goodness, thank you so much!"

I was so excited. Barb continued talking, sounding a bit bubbly.

She said, "I'll have you sign the papers. We can fax them to Mr. Brown, and you two can move in on the first of next month!"

"Barb, I appreciate all you've done to help us, and I'll see you next week."

I pressed the end button on the cordless phone and leaned against the kitchen cabinet, tracing my fingers over the buttons. I was so grateful to know that the Lord had shown us favor once again.

The call from Ron came when he finished his evening class. "Hey, baby, did you hear anything about the place yet?"

"Yes, I did. We got it!" I said happily. "Ron, there's a master bedroom with a full bath and another full bath off the hall. It has a huge guest bedroom that we can figure out what we want to do with!" I told him with such enthusiasm, he forgot about how exhausted he was.

"Well, Jeannie, when I get home, we'll have to celebrate."

"I'd like that, honey. Give me a call later after you get some rest."

Even though it was only eight o'clock, I knew there was a possibility that it might not happen even as he told me, "I'm going to call you in about an hour. I've just got to rest for a while. If you happen to keep sleeping, call me in the morning."

"Okay. Good night, sweetheart."

***

Ron shared many of his experiences with me about his days at Ball State. He told me, "Years ago, Mama used to get a call from me almost every other week talking about how I couldn't handle school anymore and how I wanted to come home. She would say, 'Alright, son. I can't come until the weekend, but if you can wait, I'll come get you then.' I didn't know until I had finished school that she was never really planning to come pick me up. It was just a way to make me stay." He laughed and then said, "I'm so grateful to her and thankful for her wisdom."

Now it was my turn to encourage Ron. The classes were getting more difficult, and he appeared to be questioning his own abilities.

He asked, "Jean, what do I think I'm doing? I've been out of school for twenty years. I can do just fine without this degree."

"Ron, you've made it through one year. I really don't want to hear this. You tell yourself daily, 'I can do all things through Christ Jesus, who strengthens me,' and if you don't know it, say it until you believe it."

Lisa gave birth to her third child as my son-in-law stood beside her bed gently rubbing her hand. "One big push," the doctor said, and in seconds, little Nidjah Nicole entered the hearts of everyone around her. After the nurse washed and dressed her in a soft pink gown, she was laid on her mommy's chest to start the bonding process. The inspection began, first counting the fingers, then the toes. Mom and Dad both agreed that she was perfect as Lisa pulled back the blanket to reveal a head full of hair. Jerry took her in his arms and gave her a proud daddy's smile.

The family was filled with excitement, but none of us was more thrilled than their four children—little Jerry, Jayla, Courdney, and Jasmine—who were waiting at home for their sister. I rewound the hands of time to when Jasmine was little and she would say, "Come on, Granny; let's sing with Barney." She'd sing, "I love you/You love me/We're a happy family/With a great big hug and a kiss from me to you/Won't you say you love me too?" I remembered how that always made me smile.

Arnetta gave birth to Amareca Patrice about three months later, and we all knew that she was here only by the grace of God. Her weight was two pounds and eight ounces. That information alone told us that she would have to be put in an incubator for a while. There were also times when she would stop breathing, so the nurses were monitoring her closely. Jackie and Sharon, Arnetta's best friends were right there along with Dora and me for her birth. As soon as we knew all was well with baby and mother, we went on a little shopping spree. Arthur came to see her, and with a really big grin, he said, "She's so little, I can hold her in one hand!"

We adored Amareca. She was everyone's baby, including Myra, who was her first babysitter when Arnetta went back to work. We watched over her, dressed in her little baby doll outfits and Pampers, and lavished her with so much love, how could she not heal?

Ron was a bit more nervous around her. "She's so tiny. . . . Just give her to me in her seat. That way I know I won't hurt her."

Our baby sister had given birth to her first child, and as I rocked the infant slowly, I thought, *If only your grandma Pearline were here, you'd be her baby too. Oh, how she would spoil you, little Amareca.*

Chapter 18

Lifting the Fog

Ninety-nine balloons would be dancing across the ceiling at the pavilion I rented for what I hoped would be a graduation celebration Ron would never forget. One hundred and ten invitations had been mailed, the decorations had been purchased, and the sheet cake had been ordered. Arnetta, along with party planner extraordinaire Jackie, made sure the food was picked up and stored in the guest room until it was time to prepare it for the party.

My weekender was packed, so everything else could wait. "I'm on my way to Rustin to get my husband!" I exclaimed.

The car was more peaceful now that we were on the highway. There was only the sound of the CD playing Margret's jams for the road. I relaxed and let my thoughts of the past years replay in my mind. They say the first five years of marriage are the most difficult. Ron was a real ladies' man, and I knew it even though he wouldn't admit it. Question him all you want, but the answer would always be the same: "It wasn't me. I didn't do it, and you know I didn't see it!" That's right; he could have been a prisoner because he was always innocent right to the bitter end.

Ron was a free spirit. He loved to travel, party, and occasionally partake in whatever made him feel even more free. He would always say, "Jean, I'm so self-destructive. You're the best woman I could ever have, and yet I'm about to lose you."

I would say, "Ron, you can't act like you're married when it's convenient and single when it's not. Doesn't our marriage deserve one hundred percent?"

For the first time, I believed I felt pain that he couldn't conceive. I was ashamed to admit it, but he was right; he was destroying our marriage and I didn't know how to handle it.

After one particularly difficult night, I packed my clothes as quickly as possible and got a Greyhound bus to Aunt Lee's house without saying a word to anyone. Ron had gone to party with some friends and decided not to come home until the next morning. If this was what our marriage was to be like, I knew I couldn't take it anymore. Somehow, he was under the impression that he could play the role of a husband when it was convenient for him, and when it wasn't, being a "grown-ass man" was supposed to make all his actions acceptable. My Aunt Lee loved Ron and believed we were good for each other. My visit with her wasn't long because each time he called, she would insist that I talk to him.

Three days later, Ron and Lorenzo were there to bring me back home. That was our first separation, and it was a week that I'll never forget and that I never want to experience again.

Margret had made the trip earlier in the year to Rustin when Ron had to come home. A piece of his disc in his lower back had broken off and was lying on his sciatic nerve. He couldn't sit and didn't have the strength in his leg to walk. The pain was excruciating, and nothing he did gave him any relief. The doctor at the hospital in Rustin had given his diagnosis and told him the piece had to be removed in order to regain full use of the leg.

"I can't believe I've come this far to have this happen. What if I can't get my degree?" Ron was angry, worried, frustrated, in pain, and a bit loopy from the medication.

We had a really good nurse practitioner who had provided our medical care for years, so when I called her after office hours, she simply said, "Don't worry; I have a really good friend I can refer Ron to as soon as he gets home. I hate to think of him being in so much discomfort." I made sure to thank her and relayed the good news to Ron.

There are times when you don't know what to say or do, and that time was now. Ron had started drifting off to sleep, so we said our goodbyes and hung up the phone. He had asked me to call President Maurer of the NFB earlier, and when I got no answer, I left him a short message asking if he could give me any advice. I prayed he would have the answer as he so often did.

It wasn't long before the phone rang again. This time it was Dr. Maurer. "Now, Jean, I got your message. I think he will heal better at home with you after his surgery, so find out what the cost is for him to fly home."

I replied, "Sir, he can't sit up, and they said if he gets a flight, he would have to purchase three seats in a row and one additional seat for a nurse."

Dr. Maurer continued in his usual calm yet sympathetic tone. "Jean, if you can't get him home any other way, call me and I'll get him home, This is not something you need to worry about."

"Sir, thank you," I replied with a sigh of relief because I knew we could depend on him to do whatever needed to be done.

The phone rang again just as I walked away from the table with all the papers I had accumulated on it from calling the train station, airports, and car rental companies.

"Hello, Jean," I heard Ron saying before I could get the phone to my ear.

"Ron, what's wrong?"

"Nothing, baby. I just wanted to tell you that Margret and Donnie are coming to get me."

After surgery and two months of exercise to strengthen his lower back and leg muscles, once again Ron was leaving for another flight to Rustin.

"This is my last quarter, Jeannie, and I'll be finished. I can't quit now," he said.

"Who said anything about you quitting? Man, you've been gone too long to be talking about coming back here without your degree. Just hurry home, Ron. This place is awfully lonely without you."

We wrapped our arms around each other, not saying another word. It was moments like this that couples hope for in a marriage, times when they can hold each other tight and no words are necessary to express the emotions inside.

It never ceases to amaze me how pointing out the things someone else does that you don't like will make you reevaluate your own life and perhaps even conclude that you also need to make a change or two. I began to separate my anger from my pain. It was clear to me that there were two different categories I needed to address and that the least of my troubles were with Ron. Yeah, sometimes we got angry with each other, but our love always brought us right back to our senses.

I felt that I had failed my daughters when their dad left because our family would not be together. I didn't want them to be separated from each other or from me. I never wanted them to feel the hurt I had felt as a child. "I know he loves them," I told my mama, "and I wouldn't say anything to change their love for him. Mama, every day with my girls is a special day that we'll never have again. I want them to always have that special bond that we didn't get to experience with Dad, and it affected each one of us deeply."

I reflected back to when I'd done my last fashion show and posed for the camera one final time. While posing, I thought of Evelyn, my former modeling coach, saying, "A model's composite sheet should tell a story if there are enough pictures, so tell your story, Jean." I posed for a trifold and told my story. My composite sheet featured me wearing glamourous, playful evening and sporty wear. I finished with a centerfold that the agency and photographer were proud of. I did several more shows and even orchestrated the stage setting for a few of them, but they were not jobs through an agency, and that made a huge difference to me. How do you just give up on something you've worked so hard to get? There was no answer that could console me, so I decided to try to move on, hoping that one day I would find something else I wanted to pour myself into.

I shifted my weight on the seat, realizing I hadn't moved an inch in a while, so my butt was getting a tingling feeling in it that went down my thigh and leg. I leaned a little to massage my calf.

I guess that was when Margret noticed I was awake and she asked, "Jean, do you need to get out and stretch? There's a rest stop coming up."

"Yes, I would. I think I sat in one position for too long."

"I'll be turning off the highway in a minute."

We were on our way to Ron's graduation. We pulled into the rest stop and took some time to stretch our legs, use the restroom, and go into the mini-mart to get snacks and drinks for the rest of the trip. I made sure to get some of Ron's favorites. I put my elbow on the armrest and rode for miles listening to Luther, then Maze and Sade's music, which was a real smooth groove, soft and low. The music was so relaxing, as if it were whispering, "No worries allowed."

During the time it took to get there, I decided to follow the little voice inside of me that was telling me to let go and let God. I felt reassured that although I knew it wouldn't go away all at once, if I let a little go at a time, the pain would eventually be no more than an insignificant memory of the past.

I let out a very slow breath and thought to myself, *Things don't always go the way I want them to go, but I'm not the one in control.* I imagined God holding me in His arms as He spoke to every one of my fears, dried my tears, and began repairing and replacing pieces of my heart that I had found discomfort in owning. I didn't know what to say, how to show my gratitude, or if words would even be enough. I knew He knows my heart, and for that I have always been thankful to God.

Ron was so excited to see all of us. Mom, Shonda, and our two nieces Tawana, and Ashley drove separately but had made the trip as well. We walked around and toured the campus, where we were introduced to Ron's instructors, colleagues, and friends. This little town had been home for Ron for almost two years, and I knew if nothing else, he was going to miss hanging out with the gang at Ponchatoulas in Louisiana. He called home some evenings just to let me know he wouldn't be in until later because he and the fellas were going to have a few cold brews. I'd get a call hours later with him laughing at something Eddie, Ruby, or Roland had done. Ron was going to miss those good times with his friends. "Nobody gets in a rush in Rustin," he said. "You can call a cab, which usually is a shared ride, and even after I'd requested an ETA, they would say with a southern drawl, 'Don't worry; we'll get ya.'"

The graduation celebration turned out just as I had planned it. All but three of the guests invited were there to share in an evening of sheer fun. It was indeed worth all the effort it took to keep the party a surprise. Family and friends came from Memphis, Arkansas, Chicago, Gary, and of course from all over Indy to share in the joy of Ron's accomplishments. I smiled at him as he told Mom, "You know Jeannie loves surprising me." It was strange that he would say that considering how much he enjoyed every one of them.

Mom was delighted at the paths her children had taken, and soon both LaTonya and Stephanie had earned their master's degree as well. Ron and I were so happy for the two of them because of the difference it would make in their careers.

Chapter 19

Valued Times

It was only natural for me and Pat to become close friends. After all, Paul and Ron were like brothers. The more time we spent with each other, the more she began to open up to me about her life.

"Jean, I don't know what's wrong with me."

"What do you mean?" I asked with concern in my voice.

"I'm tired all the time, and sometimes I can't breathe normally," she replied. "I'm finally going in to get some tests. . . . I'm so afraid of what the doctor will say."

I tried my best to comfort her, and after all the tests were completed and the results were in, the doctor told Pat that she had sarcoidosis. I still tried my best to comfort her.

"I'm getting worse," she said tearfully. "The medical bills are piling up on Paul, and I don't know what to do. Jean, I don't want to leave my son or Paul. I love them both so much. Why me, Lord? Why me?" she sobbed over the phone softly.

I searched for the right words to comfort her, but she quickly broke the silence. "The four of us have had some good times together, and I'm so thankful for that," she said through her tears.

"Yes, Pat," I said. "So are we. You will always be dear to us." I tried to keep my composure, but she knew me well enough to know that the tears were streaming down my face. I mentioned the plans we had made to ride the South Shore train to Chicago.

"We were going to make a day of it," Pat said.

"We can still have lunch and walk around downtown for a while. Then we can get dinner and go to a concert," I said.

"That sounds like a plan. We can celebrate Paul's birthday and Valentine's Day together."

We spent the rest of the call making more plans that we could only pray to see come to pass.

A few days later, Pat was admitted to the hospital. "They say I have an infection. Jean, I've never felt this bad before. I just want to go home," she said in a very soft, wishful tone.

Pat's voice was weak, and all I wanted was for her to stay strong and not lose her faith. "Don't worry; you'll be home soon."

I thought back on the night that I convinced Pat to let me help her reupholster her kitchen chairs. It took about five hours, but with the new Babyface CD playing her favorite song "Every Time I Close My Eyes" repeatedly, we got the job done.

"That's my song to my baby," she said as she sipped on her glass of wine.

The days went by with some improvement, and I thought Pat was regaining her strength, but she only got better to get worse. Neither of us wanted to admit it out loud, but our plans for a day in the city would not come to pass.

We went to Gary to her homegoing service and did everything in our power to comfort Paul and her son, but we knew it would take time to heal their broken hearts.

"Paul, you know if you need us, we're only a phone call away. I have to be at the business Monday, but I'll be in touch," Ron said as we hugged Paul and said our goodbyes.

Our house wasn't completely furnished yet, so some rooms had furniture while others were practically empty except for the carpet on the floor and the blinds that covered the windows in each room. In all the years of our marriage, Ron had never made me a promise that he didn't keep, so I had no reason to ever doubt him. When he was away at school, he had told me that he was going to buy me a house, and I would never have to move again unless I wanted. Here we were living in a quiet neighborhood not far from the apartment complex we once lived in. It was a beautiful ranch-style house with everything we were looking for in a home. There was a fireplace in the family room, a guest room, and lots of yard space. There was plenty of room for the two of us, and I thought about how it was such a blessing to be sitting across the table from the man that I adored each day.

Ron opened the window over the desk in the kitchen and came back to the table to sit again. He waited patiently for his breakfast while listening to the radio and sipping on his cup of hot coffee. With the window opened a couple of inches, there was a slight chill still in the air that teased us in the mornings for several weeks here in the Midwest, but it was definitely going to be a beautiful spring day. I set a plate on the placemat with bacon, cheesy eggs, a bowl of grits, and Texas toast and turned to walk away, asking him "Do you need anything else?"

Ron hesitated before answering me, then replied, "Come, eat with me. I'm not going to eat without you."

With a smile, I told him, "I'll be right there."

We were both morning people, and having breakfast together was like an old tradition I would never want to break. No matter how simple the breakfast was, it was complete when Ron made that superb pot of coffee. And there was something special about the little kiss on the jaw he gave me after a meal. The words "thank you" could never leave the lasting pleasure that his kisses did.

The cane travel business was picking up for Ron. His name was spreading like wildfire in the blind community across the state of Indiana. Business counselors wanted to contract his services. Yes, Cane and Able Orientation and Mobility Services had made it! It didn't matter if the person was deaf, blind, in a wheelchair, walking with the use of a walker, multiply disabled with blindness, visually impaired, or totally blind; it was Ron's goal to build the person's confidence and teach him or her every skill needed to traverse the world.

"Jean, you know I get so much satisfaction from teaching cane travel. I like the vending business, but I feel as though I'm fulfilling my purpose when I help someone with a disability do what comes naturally for me, teaching them how to be independent." There was something about the smile I imagined on his face. This business truly made him happy. No, it was more than that. It made his self-worth skyrocket, and I was a witness to the journey God was taking him on.

Ron was running the dishwater when I looked across the room at him and said, "I'm going to church tomorrow. Would you like to go?"

"No, not tomorrow. Maybe next time," he said evasively as he continued to wash the dishes.

"Ron, you cannot outrun God," I said, as I had so many times before.

I gave the drying towel a quick twist and popped him on his behind. A smile came on my lips as I dried the dishes and thought to myself, *God, does he know yet that his life is not his own? I can't wait to see what you have in store for him!*

***

What do you do when the president of the National Federation of the Blind tells you to come to his office after general session is adjourned? *You freak out!* Yep, that's exactly what he did.

Ron was a ball of nerves as he declared, "I'm as nervous as a long-tail cat in a roomful of rocking chairs. What did I do wrong? Is there something I'm not doing in our state?"

He was on a roll, and before he asked another question that he didn't pause long enough to let me answer, I said, "Stop worrying. You didn't do anything wrong. Maybe he has some suggestions for you as state president. RB, just chill. Everything's alright," I said to him as he continued to pace the floor until time to leave out and make it to the president's suite.

As it turned out, Ron had done nothing wrong but everything right! The nominating committee had placed his name on the ballot, and our federation family elected him to serve as a member of the national board. This was such a surprise!

"Jean, sometimes you do the work just because you believe in something, not because you expect to get something in return. I didn't even know that Dr. Maurer was considering me for a board position, but I won't let him or the federation down."

"I know you won't," I said.

Ron continued in total amazement of his victory. "You and I agree that it's not the title that keeps us committed to this organization. The National Federation of the Blind is not just a way in life; it has become a way of life. I'm so glad Dr. Maurer came to our campus and got me and Paul to join the federation because it has changed my life, and I could never repay him for that."

***

Lisa, once more, and Latrice brought our families two little bundles of joy, born just months apart.

Lisa decided on the name Jaden Ronald. She said that after giving Courdney her daddy's name for his middle name, they decided to give Jaden Ron's name for his middle name. Ron was as proud as he could be. "Thanks, Lisa, for naming him after me."

"You've been in my life since I was nine years old. You are my daddy too," Lisa told him, sounding pleased with their decision.

The one thing that I couldn't give Ron was a son who would have his name, his good looks, and his talents. Not being able to give to him a son tore at my heart for many years. I knew what it was like to lose a child, but to not have the ability to have our own son some days seemed so cruel. The words never formed on my lips, but my mind insisted on replaying the pain, and I prayed that the pain didn't touch the heart of the man I loved so deeply. I believe God heard and delivered right on time; now we have the joy of our grandchildren all around us to brighten our days. Each one adds his or her own special touch to our lives.

Latrice gave birth to Kaitlin Simone. She was her first child, and even though the delivery was a difficult one, the doctor informed us that mother and baby were doing just fine. Edward was there smiling with a look of unbelief that the two of them had created such a beautiful baby girl. Kaitlin's Grandma Sue and Auntie Lisa were there. Everyone was excited.

Lisa said, "Oh, Mama, she looks like a little mini-Latrice."

Sue threw her arms around me in excitement. "She's beautiful, Jean!" I couldn't physically see the baby, but I didn't doubt that at all. It was so touching to see my baby holding her baby girl, giving so much love and affection.

When I started working again after our final move, I held a front desk receptionist position. I enjoyed the job and interacting with my coworkers. However, I came to the conclusion that I had to establish a new career for myself, and I wasn't going to be intimidated because of my blindness. I attended a business conference with Ron for the vending program, and the guest speaker said the acronym FEAR stood for "false emotions appearing real." With that word of encouragement, I knew that fear would not stop me from reaching my destination. I remembered Aunt Lee's words when she told me, "What God has for you is for you, and no one else can claim it."

Yes, I was ready to move forward. It proved to be a challenging task to work a forty-hour week, take care of my home, and write a business plan, but I was thankful that Mr. Moneymaker, my employer, allowed me the opportunity to stay on with Fridays off so I could make business calls. He changed the schedule to a thirty-two-hour week until my plan was complete.

I knew I would miss my coworker Kim and our afternoon talks. She was always so genuine and easy to talk to. She taught me so much on the job as a receptionist—all the skills I would need to manage my business I had decided to open. I understood for the first time the importance of each job I had taken in life and could now appreciate how each one was preparing me for something more.

Ron tried not to complain, but on nights that I stayed in our home office until three or four in the morning, he would get up and say, "That's enough, Jean. Come to bed and start again tomorrow."

"I'm going to get a nap later on today," I would say as I snuggled next to him. "I love you. Good night."

***

Time has a way of flying not only when you're having fun, but especially when you're trying to get a little sleep. I sat up on the side of the bed and pushed the alarm button down just as the clock was about to sound off for the third time, informing me that it was five a.m. I was determined to meet the deadline I had set for myself, and my persistence had paid off.

It's amazing what can be accomplished when the support system that's behind you keeps pushing you forward, creating the momentum needed to succeed. I had a vision that I wanted to become a reality, and my brother helped by drawing the logo for my business. Lisa and Latrice made sure the décor was all I wanted it to be as we traveled from one side of town to the other, comparing styles as well as prices and quality. Everything was perfect. The selections could not have been better. I woke up each morning with so much gratitude to God and my entire family. I felt in that moment that it had to be that cloud nine experience I'd heard about. When you meet a very special goal in your life, it feels like you've just floated away on a cloud.

Mom started working as my assistant, and the times we had together meant so much to me. Each day gave me the opportunity to get to know her even more, and what I found out was just how much more incredible she was than I'd known. Her honesty in every situation concerning each person hired could never be diminished even when it applied to me. I have so much love and respect for her. Her small frame moved gracefully from one room to another, periodically stopping at her desk to take a call for an appointment or grab her notepad.

Mom's style caught the attention of many eyes, male and female alike. Whatever she wore had to be classy or jazzy with a touch of elegance that finalized her fashion statement. I was certain that no one could ever replace her or the love she gave so freely. *It's no wonder I call her Mom*, I thought as we sat in my office reviewing the stack of applications from the file cabinet to schedule more interviews. It would have been extremely difficult to manage the business without her, and not nearly as much fun.

Every year the National Federation of the Blind national president sends members of the national board to a state convention to represent the organization, and as Ron traveled from state to state, I was by his side. It was an honor and a privilege to serve the federation to impart the knowledge and wisdom we had gained during our many years as members and as leaders.

It was work, but we definitely made the most of our fun federation trips. We would always make time for a trip to the local casino, a walk, a bowl-a-thon, or even a dinner at a nice restaurant. Just say the word "fun," and you can count us in! Please don't think being blind means boredom because it doesn't. When you lose your sight, it's not a death sentence. It's your new life. Go ahead and make the most of it!

It's so exciting to have new additions to the family, and so we welcomed Samari Jayani with love and open arms. Lisa was the perfect mother to all of her children, and I loved seeing her flourish in her role. After Samari was born, Lisa told us that her newest baby would have to stay in the hospital for a while due to her swallowing some fluids during the birth. The whole family rallied together in prayer for the newest baby. We knew the Lord would heal her.

Lisa was as concerned as ever, but I knew she had a lot of faith in the Lord, and all we needed to do was trust in His holy word. Lisa stayed at the hospital to avoid the twenty-minute drive if she needed to come back in a hurry, while Jerry stayed at home and made sure all the children got off to school each day. Ron and I were so relieved when we got Lisa's call saying, "Mama, she pooped out most of the bilirubin and soaked the entire pad! They want to keep her one more day for observation, but we will be going home tomorrow!" Lisa was physically drained, but she held onto her belief, and her prayers were answered.

Ron was waiting for me to hang up the phone so I could give him the update, and when I did, he replied, "God is good."

"Yes, indeed He is, and we will be able to see her very soon," I told Ron. "She's healthy. Thank God our grands are healthy!"

***

The Indy Thunder Beep Baseball Team was working extremely hard to build a team that would be unstoppable. Some of the veterans on the team knew how sweet the taste of victory was, but those who were younger knew only the taste of defeat, and it was a bitter pill to swallow. They wanted more, but first the desire to win, to be the champions, just had to become a reality.

A banquet was held for the players who were being inducted into the Beep Baseball Hall of Fame, and Ron stepped up proudly to receive his recognition. Booker, the man who wore many hats on the team, one of which included team manager, surprised Ron with a shadowbox that held a beep baseball and the retired jersey number 25.

John accompanied Mom to the dinner, and she looked on as her oldest son received his honors. He took in the sound of the cheers that filled the room, and then his voice began to quiet the crowd. "Thank you; thank you all. I'm honored that I excelled in this sport for our team. I know my number just got retired, but I think you all know I'll be here. I love you, Thunder!"

The crowd was up on their feet now, clapping and chanting, *"Thunder rolls!"*

Mom clapped and yelled out his name with so much excitement. "You go, Ron!"

When Ron was seated again beside me, I touched his hand and whispered, "Number twenty-five, win or lose, I'm honored to be your wife."

He leaned towards me, planted a kiss on my lips, and said, "Jeannie, I love you."

What an accomplishment, and if anyone else understood what this day meant to him, I was sure it was Mom. I pictured the smile on her face and the glow in her dark brown eyes as she said, "I'm so proud of you, son."

"Thank you, Mother!" he shouted, hoping to be heard over the crowd.

Paul's life was busy with his job teaching children in the Gary public school system who had a very low visual acuity or were totally blind. His goal was to enhance their blindness skills, and I'm sure he made a world of difference in his class with his positive attitude. It was quite evident that Paul didn't want to remain a bachelor, at least not long term. I don't know exactly when Paul and FaSondra started dating, but she put a sense of joy back in his life, and soon afterwards she became Mrs. Howard. Amazingly, they left Indiana and relocated to Alaska, where Paul's teaching career continued to flourish as they settled into their new home.

We missed our friends, but we kept in touch by sending text messages until we saw them again at the NFB national convention. We all remained busy with the federation, hoping that one day someone would look back at all the years devoted to the cause and say they were instrumental in the changes made for blind people everywhere.

Dr. Maurer and the first lady, Patricia, after twenty-eight years had passed on the gavel, and now Mark Riccobono was the leader, with his lovely wife, Malissa, by his side. More than two thousand people at the convention were cheering him on as he made his way to the podium to give his thanks to us for the confidence and belief in his abilities as our new president.

Changes were taking place everywhere, and this one filled my heart with joy the most: Ron invited me to church!

"It's time to make some changes, and I think Transforming Life Church is where we need to be," he said.

Everything in me said, *Go ahead, jump up and down, shout some words of praise. Let him know you're excited that he made this decision.* Instead I replied calmly, "Of course, I'd love to go with you to church."

Ron turned up the volume a little to finish watching a movie while I sat on the love seat beside him and thought to myself, *All things in God's time, Ron Brown . . . all things.*

The doors were locked for the last time on a business I worked so hard to build, and the tears fell with every thought of my lost enterprise. I cried myself to sleep quietly most nights for a while, and I tried instinctively to wear a smile. Suddenly my tears were falling on my scrambled cheese eggs as I tried to explain to Ron how I felt about the salon and day spa closing.

Ron put his fork down, came to my chair, held me close, and said, "It's alright, Jean. You did everything you could. There's no need to cry anymore."

That morning, all the pain, anger, and disappointment I had been feeling vanished. Somehow I felt relieved. How could this be? I asked Myra, who had become more than my stylist but a very close friend.

"I don't know, Jean, but you will find something else to do if you don't open another spa. Just give it some time. You'll figure it out."

Ron remained the second vice president of the National Federation of the Blind, and with his serving as an officer in the organization, we traveled to many conventions, where he served as the national representative. Every state holds many special memories, but some stood out more than others. In New York we enjoyed the stage play *The Phantom of the Opera*, where we had second- and third-row seats for members of the federation. Hawaii is an island of beauty. They have a way of sharing the customs and traditions with the visitors of their island that will have you pleading for more!

The beauty of Alaska is the wildlife, the mountains, and the ocean. Ron and I found our way to one of the world's largest malls in Anchorage. With our canes in hand, we had people holding their breath as we took the escalators and wandered in and out of stores until we were ready to return to the hotel.

In Puerto Rico, we experienced the beauty of the island and the sincere kindness of its people. Ron pointed out to me the two different textures in the concrete pavement, so we were able to follow what we called the yellow brick road until we got to the souvenir shop. Of course, none of this was done without people following behind us watching us, some stopping us along the way because they thought we were lost.

I'm not sure which state I enjoyed most because they were all so unique and different compared to the Midwest. However, Ron had always had his heart set on a move to Arizona. I think I could learn to like that! During the years we have traveled, our federation family has grown, and any introduction to a new person is an opportunity to increase our extended family.

Like any other day, while Ron prepared himself for work, I cooked our breakfast and served a cup of hot coffee to him and Arthur. We talked about what had been going on in our lives. Ron and I had returned home from Florida, where we had attended the World Blind Union Conference. Arthur had made it to Indy two days prior to our returning. He had come to visit from North Carolina. It had been a few years since we had seen him, and we were enjoying catching up with one another.

Ron made it to work and called me as he did every morning. "Hey, baby, I'm at work now, and the crowd is coming in, so I'd better go make the coffee. I'll call you in a little while. I love you."

I gave my usual, "Alright, I'll talk to you later. I love you too." I placed the phone on the kitchen counter and stacked the dirty dishes in the sink.

"Good morning!" my grandson Courdney said as he walked into the kitchen.

Arthur and I both spoke, and, as with grandmas everywhere, my first question was to ask him if he wanted some food. He declined, telling me he would have something later in the day, and continued out to the front porch, talking on his phone.

Arthur called to me, "Hey, Jean, come here. Let me read this scripture to you."

"Okay, Arthur. I'll be there in a minute. If you're done with the coffee, I'm going to turn off the pot now."

"Two cups are enough for me right now," he answered.

There was no sign of rain just minutes before. The sudden roll of thunder across the sky had all of my attention focused on the weather conditions. I unplugged the coffee maker and the microwave, then turned the lights off in the kitchen and dining room. We certainly had seen worse rainstorms than this, but the sound of the thunder rolling as it reached its destination had the windows and the foundation shaking.

I called to Arthur, "Tell Courdney to come in now!" He heard the urgency in my voice and didn't say a word. He went to the front porch, and in seconds the two of them came back in the house.

My brother entered the family room where I had gone to turn the television off. He said, "Jean, it's just a thunderstorm. Don't worry."

I moved to the dining room, where I could hear the sirens going off in the distance. I'd been here through many storms, but never had I heard one like this. I rushed to my bedroom to turn the television off and grabbed the remote. As I pressed the off button, the house shook, and I fell on the bed. There was the sound of glass breaking. Something had just hit the house! What could it have been? I wondered. *Oh my God! Arthur was in there sitting in my recliner.*

I ran down the hallway to the dining room and called out to him, "Arthur, where are you?

Are you alright?"

He responded in a very low tone, "I'm in the laundry room. Something hit my head." He sounded confused and in pain. As I turned to walk towards the family room, he called out to me, saying, "Don't go in there, Jean. There are sparks everywhere. The electrical lines are down, and a tree is in the family room."

Dear Lord, it was not even fifteen minutes ago that it was peaceful and quiet in our neighborhood, and now . . . I shivered at the thought of what had happened. Taking a step back away from what used to be our family room and with tears in my eyes, I thought, *How could this happen?*

"Arthur, what are we going to do?"

"Get some shoes on. We've got to get out of here quick! Where is your medicine? Jean, don't forget to get your purse."

Courdney had called Lisa, and I could hear him explaining, "Mama, a tree just fell on Granny's house. I'm standing in the driveway, and you can see the top of the tree in the front yard, and the roots are above ground in the backyard. I've never seen anything like this."

I wasn't sure, but I had a feeling Courdney was in shock. I looked up at the dining room ceiling, and I could hear it cracking, making what was a fraction of an inch–wide turn into a much wider opening as the insulation fell to the floor from the attic. The cracks stretched across the ceiling in more than one place, and the rain poured into the house.

I called my husband and explained the situation.

"Are you all alright?"

"Yes," I said again, but my heart was pounding much too fast.

I heard Arthur in the other room saying, "Jean, come on. I don't know if the house is going to collapse or not!"

Ron was still on the phone in disbelief over what happened as well and said, "I'll be home as soon as I can get there. All of you are safe, and that's all that matters."

The rain suddenly stopped, and it was your usual August day with a few exceptions: a tree was in our home, which made it unsafe to stay there, and every room in the house was damaged to some degree except the room Courdney was staying in. It wasn't long before Latrice drove up, and minutes later Ron had been finally able to make it around the areas that looked like a war zone in our neighborhood.

We packed as much as possible, leaving much more then we wanted to, but we had each other, and we were thankful for that. We were thankful for our friends and family who came over and offered us whatever they thought would help us through this horrifying ordeal.

Donnie and Arthur stayed at the house with Ron as long as they could, but the rain continued to fall throughout the evening, flooding the streets in nearby neighborhoods. At Latrice's house, I kneeled in the guest room at the side of the bed to pray, realizing that sometimes only a few words are needed. I said, "Lord, thank you for your mercy and grace."

We settled into a hotel suite. Our routine picked back up again, and our love stood stronger than ever. The old three-ton oak tree made walls crumble around us, but God in His infinite wisdom said, "Peace, be still," and calmed the storms both in us and around us.

Epilogue

Our home was rebuilt over the next eight months, and we realized that sometimes you have to adapt to the changes, pick up the pieces, and move on. The world won't stop turning even when your life is coming unglued. Ron continued to work both his vending business and his orientation and mobility business, Cane and Able, and both continue to thrive. My fundraising efforts had to continue for the federation, and all the responsibilities we took on had to be completed.

We took an Uber to church on Sundays, where Pastor Chris blessed us with his prayers and the word of God, which kept us grounded as the months went by while we waited to return home. Pastor Kim and the choir always lifted our spirits with beautiful songs of praise that filled the sanctuary.

The workout room at the hotel suite during our time away from home helped us focus on our health, and when we got stir-crazy in the hotel, Pam and Toney invited us over for a weekend sleepover. Dining out with friends and family was a pleasure that made hotel living more like being at home.

There was a chill in the air now, reminding me of the frosty season that was upon us.

"Mom, put your phone on speaker so Ron can hear too. Would you like to go to Florida with us for Christmas?" Lisa said one evening during one of our usual chats. "It will be so much fun. A hotel is no place to be on a holiday." The vacation was much needed and totally enjoyed!

We often have to answer many questions to give insight on how we manage activities of daily living skills such as cooking, daily household chores, parenting, education, transportation for employment and travel. With no doubts in our mind, we knew we would have to answer the questions many would ask, and that's alright because the life you live should be a learning experience, one filled with lots of hopes, dreams, and promises, and lots of questions. We have and continue to make strides daily to break down barriers for the blind and disabled community and the community as a whole. While we continue to aspire to achieve our hopes, and dreams, we embrace the questions that will allow us to continue to contribute and work in communities across the world.

The last chapter of this book has not been written yet, for if it had been, I would be deceased, and I am very much alive, living my best destiny.

Special Memories!!

Bachelor of Science, 1980
Margaret E. Fairbairn Award
Distinguished Award Center for Leadership Development, 1989
Master of Arts in Educational Psychology – Orientation & Mobility, 1999
Ivy Tech State College on-the-job trainer for Randolph Sheppard Vending Program, 2002
NBBA, numerous trophies, awards, and medals
Indy Thunder NBBA Hall of Famer, 2011
Jacobus Tenbroek Award, 2015, National Federation of the Blind highest honor (Ron and Jean)
NBBA World Series Champions, 2016, Indy Thunder
NBBA World Series Champions, 2017, Indy Thunder

Lisa Wilson, RN (she is continuing her education and pursuing a business opportunity)
Latrice Jeter, Simplified Insurance Solution LLC (accounting degree, business administration degree, and owner/CEO of SIS LLC)
Arnetta Williams (accounting degree, education degree, furthering her studies)
Katrina Brown-Patterson (writer, business degree)
LaTonya Brown (accounting degree, currently a CFO in North Carolina)
Stephanie Brown (master's degree in business)

www.ingramcontent.com/pod-product-compliance
Lightning Source LLC
Chambersburg PA
CBHW020415080526
44584CB00014B/1337